INDOOR GARDENING

INDOOR GARDENING

INDOOR GARDENING

Growing Herbs, Greens, & Vegetables Under Lights

The Hungry Garden series #4

Rosefiend Cordell

INDOOR GARDENING

Rosefiend Publishing.

Ordering information: For details, contact the publisher at hello@melindacordell.com
Cover design by Melinda R. Cordell
Book formatting by Melinda R. Cordell

Amazon ISBN: 978-1-953196-62-0

First Edition: January 2023

10 9 8 7 6 5 4 3 2 1 blast off!

MELINDA R. CORDELL
AUTHOR & GARDENING WRITER

For more information (and books!), visit my website at
https://melindacordell.com/

**Subscribe to my Newsletter
and get <u>a free gardening book</u>.**

The Hungry Garden Series

Big Yields, Little Pots – Container Gardening for the Creative Gardener
Book 1

Edible Landscaping – Foodscaping and Permaculture for Urban Gardeners
Book 2

Beneficial and Pest Insects – The Good, the Bad, and the Hungry
Book 3

Indoor Gardening – Growing Herbs, Greens, & Vegetables Under Lights
Book 4

FORTHCOMING BOOKS!

Growing a Food Forest – Trees, Shrubs, & Perennials That'll Feed Ya!
Book 5

Wildscaping – Using Native Food Plants to Create a Ecologically-Friendly Garden
Book 6

Survival Rations! – Foraging in Wild Spaces for Greens, Berries, & Nuts
Book 7

Victory Gardens – We Can Grow It!
Book 8

Tiny-Space Vegetable Gardening – Making the Best of Garden Spaces
Book 9

Just to say 'Thank You' for purchasing this book, I want to give you a gift 100% absolutely free.

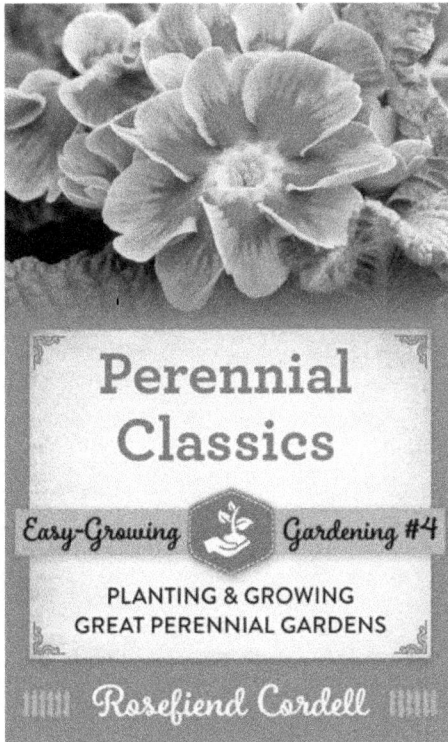

Perennial Classics: Planting & Growing Great Perennial Gardens from my Easy-Growing Gardening series.

Click here to get your free book!
https://melindacordell.com/subscribe/

INDOOR GARDENING

ACKNOWLEDGEMENTS

A hearty tip o' the pen to Keith Rhodes, who took on this manuscript when it was still a wreck with parts strewn all over the place and gave me a hand with edits. Thank you so much. Hopefully this endeavor has not permanently turned you away from editing for good!

THE·TABLE·OF CONTENTS

INDOOR GARDENING

INTRODUCTION

This book is focused on growing edible plants inside in containers under natural light and artificial lights.

Poor lighting isn't always apparent to the layman's eye. When I started growing indoor plants, I bought a bunch of random grow lights, not knowing how to do this lighting thing. I tried different lights with different plants, mixed them around. I noticed that some of my setups were great while others didn't work, but I thought that overall the plants were fine.

However, I didn't realize that my light source was mediocre until I noticed that none of my orchids were blooming even though it was winter (their usual bloom time). I despaired of ever seeing my mystery orchid blooming.

But I finally improved my lighting setup. When I put my mystery orchid underneath an LED red and blue light, that plant finally took off … and put out the biggest flower spike I've ever seen!

Sometimes it takes a little while to figure out what kinds of light works best for your plants. And that's okay.

Now I'm paying closer attention to how my plants react to the lights, adjust them and moving them around to see where the plants seem the happiest.

Indoor gardening is like that. A lot of trial and error is involved. But it's a fun way to spend time, but more importantly, it's also a way to improve your life when nutritious produce is selling for sky-high prices. If you can find out how to grow a some leafy vegetables such as lettuce, kale, or bok choy under lights, or grow your own sprouts, and even a tomato plant, you can supplement your diet with nourishing produce, and you can also have more choice in the types of lettuce you grow – because now you can branch out into heirloom varieties that are eye-catching and tasty.

Certain herbs are easy to grow inside. You can grow carrots, beet greens, even strawberries with the right light and potting media. You're not going to be able to grow huge quantities of them, but they can improve the quality of your life.

*

A side note: try not to go overboard in spending a lot of money on these systems. Find out more about them before you make big purchases.

I hear about people who drop $500 on garden supplies and only end up growing a tiny squash when all is said and done. As a gal who grew up reading my grandma's old *Organic Gardening* magazines when they were still a small outfit in Vermont living the cheap gardening life, while helping my other grandma in various big gardening setups where she saved her own seeds and didn't spend money on hardly any of it, this boggles my mind.

I remember seeing my 80-something great-grandpa in the big raspberry garden pushing a small cultivator, which is basically a small plow, between the rows. Would he have used one of those gas-powered tillers if he could have afforded it? Hard to say. Grandpa was a little stubborn, but at the same time, he used what he had at hand, because we didn't have a lot of money. That's just the way it was.

So, I was raised in a tradition of gardening on a shoestring, and it's a good way for a beginner to learn. Start small and use what you have at hand as the old (we're not that old) frugal gardeners did. Then once you learn the ropes, you can scale up to buying good-quality equipment when necessary.

This photo is merely to show off my pretty Oncidium alliance orchid.

GETTING STARTED

"Honey, Where Are You Putting All These Plants?"

The problem with time and space as we know it means that we can't have a house like Dr. Who's Tardis. Outside, it looks exactly like a police box; inside, it contains 500 square miles of space, plus a pool (I actually have no idea if Dr. Who had a pool) and a room for really long scarves (for Tom Baker).

So if you're like me and you live in a house that has, and this is a rough but accurate estimate, about 25 square feet of space – then finding a place for more plants is a challenge.

Not that this has stopped me from buying more indoor plants, oh gosh no.

But if you want to grow food plants indoors, then finding a good location for them might take a little more effort. At minimum you'll need 1) a space that's large enough for them to grow to their full size 2) in a place that completely fills their light needs.

If you are design savvy, you'll also need 3) all plants and materials to be aesthetically pleasing. This book probably will not give you very much on this score, for which I'm very sorry. If I ran a home decorating show, it would pretty much consist of, "This space can be improved by piling a bunch of books on top of it, along with this cool rock I found." So I'm not exactly your go-to source for interior design inspirations.

Plants grown for food instead of aesthetics will need full light, whether from the sun or from supplemental light. A flat of lettuce can survive on the kind of light you give to a dracaena or a pothos or some other low-light houseplant – but the lettuce plant won't be happy, and it won't bear the tasty greens that you planted it for. It will be tall and leggy and sad and pale, like ghost lettuce. You don't want to make a salad that looks like Bunnicula has been raiding the vegetables in your fridge.

So, let's start with the first step of garden prep, whether that garden is inside or outside: Assessing what you have and figuring out how you can make it work.

"Honey, get those houseplants outta here! From now on this place is gonna be Tomato City!"

Assess Your Site/Window

Take a look at the space you've decided to give to your plants. If it's near a window, how much light will the window provide? Do you need to supplement that light with an artificial light source? If you do, is there a plug-in nearby? If not, do you have an extension cord long enough to reach it? And can you place that cord where nobody is going to trip over it?

I really didn't expect to have to do THAT much thinking over where to put a pot of herbs, but here we are.

But this is a big deal: Some of these plants are going to take a lot of light. I mean a LOT of light.

Higher levels of light will generally lead to higher yields for most plants, specifically, larger crops like tomatoes. However, if you're growing some lettuce and sprouts, you're not going to need to capture the entire sun and put it in your living room.

You might have to find a way to block the light from the rest of the house, like putting up a partition of some sort.

Keeping Costs Down

When it comes to costs such as grow lights, soil, shelves, and the electric bill — start small, especially if you're getting started. As any plant aficionado knows, it's easy to add to the collection but harder than heck to trim down the population once you have plants heaped upon on every lighted surface in the house. So it goes.

Start with a couple herbs and some lettuce under a cheap grow light. Put a little pot of carrots in the window. Use an old tray from a greenhouse to grow microgreens.

Instead of buying pots, poke holes at the bottom of a cottage-cheese container and use that. Old milk jugs and 2-liter pop containers, cleaned out, can serve as pots or mini-greenhouses, depending on which side you put the soil in. Rotisserie chicken containers or large containers for lettuce make instant small greenhouses.

Ever since time began, gardeners have always been saving bits of twine to tie up plants, reusing old pots, saving seeds from year to year to plant them again. Compost is reusing old scraps – you don't even have to buy a compost-turner or a fancy bin for it.

Some grow lights are pricey, so you can start with a smaller set, and put up reflective material facing the plants. This will bounce extra light back on the plants while keeping that same light out of your eyes. Some folks will set a large mirror up next to their plants, or hang several mylar space blankets around the plants, which are lightweight but marvelously reflective.

There's no shame in looking for cheap alternatives. MacGyver your garden.

What Plants Need

Now that you've found your location, let's take a moment for a quick overview of the general points of what your container-grown indoor crop plants will need to thrive.

Light – This is the big issue in indoor gardening, so I hope you'll forgive me if I save this part of the discussion for later in the book – I will be devoting several chapters to lighting, grow lamps, and a bunch of other interrelated details.

Air – Hopefully your home has air. If it doesn't, I highly recommend moving, because being able to breathe is very helpful to your quality of life!

Seriously, have some air circulation around your plants. Have a fan running to keep air moving through the plants to discourage fungal diseases.

Soil – For indoor plants, soil is replaced by soilless mixes. The potting mix you get from the store is made of mixes of light materials such as peat moss, coir, perlite, and other sterile ingredients. Get a bag of light potting mix from the store. Don't use top soil or dirt from outside, as this can bring diseases inside and will become too compacted in the pot.

Containers – Choose pots that are large enough for your plants to prosper. If you're raising seedlings, use trays that you get from the local garden center. And make sure all pots have drainage holes.

I go into a *lot* of detail about soil and containers in my other book *Big Yields, Little Pots: Container Gardening for the Creative Gardener,* so if you have any questions about soilless potting mix, the ingredients that go into it, and the wide array of pot materials that you could use, skip over and grab a copy of that book because it will load you up with all the specs.

Water – One aspect of container gardening that's often overlooked is the water. To understand why, we need to talk a little bit about plant physiology and chemistry.

Positively-charged ions draw nutrients to the plant roots. Specific nutrients (which are different chemicals) are attracted to these ions. The pH of the soil and water can affect how well these nutrients are absorbed – or can hinder them. Nutrients have pH ranges within which they're able to be absorbed. But if the soil or water are at the wrong pH, the magnetism between the nutrient and the plant root is reduced and the root cannot absorb the nutrient.

We see this in oak trees that are planted in alkaline soils. The develop a condition called chlorosis in which their leaves turn yellow-green. Chlorosis is caused by the roots not being able to absorb the iron in the alkaline soil. If the oak tree is planted in acidic soil, it's easily able to absorb the iron and the leaves are a nice green color.

If your plants seem to be struggling, you might get a pH pen and use it to check two things: The water you are using to water the plants, and the soil in the pots. Then look at the pH requirements of your plants to see if this you need to change your water or soil. You might need to use filtered water, or change your potting soil.

Don't overdo watering. It's okay to let the soil dry slightly between waterings. Seedlings and seeds should stay moist but not continually soggy.

If you have rain barrels to collect rainwater, use this to water the plants. Cities treat drinking water to make it safe to drink, adding chemical or added salts. Rainwater contains few salts or chemicals, and even contains a little nitrogen that was converted by lightning in the atmosphere, which is also good for plants.

Fertilizer – Add a granular, slow-release fertilizer to the soil before you plant your seeds. You can also fertilize the growing seedlings and grown plants with a water-soluble fertilizer every two weeks. Don't fertilize more often, as fertilizer tends to build up over time in the soil in the form of salts, and can eventually make the soil inhospitable to the plants. Fertilizer might also affects the taste and smell of some plants.

Temperature – Best at about 70 degrees. Don't place plants next to a heating or cooling source.

Humidity – Plants need humidity! During winter, indoor humidity can be as low as 20% – about the same humidity as the Sahara Desert! Use a humidifier.

Another way to raise humidity a little is by clustering plants together, as long as there's a little space between them for air circulation. Or, set the plants on a tray filled with pebbles, and pour in water to below the level of the pebbles. The evaporating water will add humidity to the air.

What Do I Want to Plant?

So why do you want to start an indoor garden? Are you tired of having to pay ten bucks for fancy lettuce? Do you want to have fresh herbs handy for cooking? Do you have no outside gardening space and it's driving you nuts? Do you like being surrounded by plants?

So what do you want to grow? What do you like to eat? If this is the first time you're indoor gardening, is there a crop you particularly enjoy? Or are you getting all worked up by looking at these heirloom seed catalogues? Because YOU WANT TO SAMPLE ALL THESE COOL LETTUCE VARIETIES! which is totally understandable.

What Stands in My Way?

Before you start, assess what could go wrong. I've discovered that when I assess all the things that could go wrong and prepare for them, none of those things happen – because something I never expected happens instead.

Are you fighting aphids or other pests/diseases on your other houseplants? Then keep your new plants away from the pest-infected plants. Keep any infected plants in strict quarantine, crush the insect rebellion – and leave them in quarantine until you're certain the insects never come back.

Do you have a cat? Cats are the indoor equivalents to squirrels. They can ruin anything. A squirrel will eat all your mulberries and apples. A cat will lie down in your tomato pot, eat your lettuce, and haul a plant out of its pot and drag it across the floor because he is offended by it. You can tell a cat NO and the cat looks at you, profoundly unimpressed.

A zillion years ago when I worked at the garden center, I brought home cuttings of plants we were throwing out, and would root them a tray of soil. But soon I noticed that the baby cuttings were looking sickly and sad. What the heck was going on? Then I came in from school one day and found my cat sitting on the tray, using it as her litter box.

So that was the end of my propagation schemes, pretty much. Thanks a lot, Ladycat!

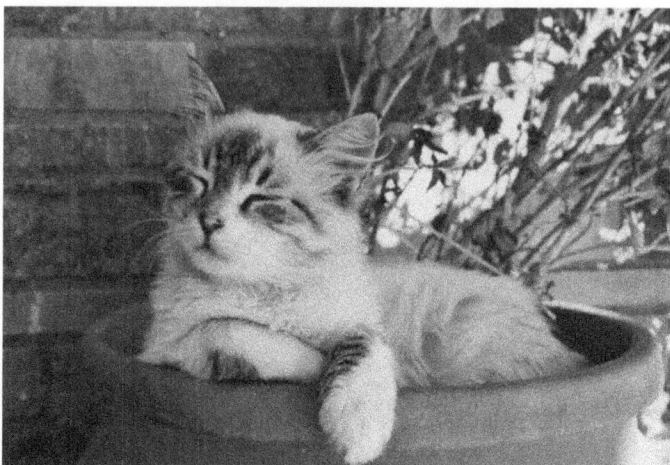

Everything you own actually belongs to your cat. (Pic by DanaTentis)

Dogs are the same way. I used to have a golden Labrador named Cricket, and in one of those rare times when she was in the house, her madly wagging tail would clear off our coffee table in seconds. If you have a dog with a happy tail, guard your plants against it.

Most dogs are fine with merely supervising you as you work with your plants, because their job is to keep an eye on you. But guard your plants against a dog that gets the zoomies and goes into hyperdrive in the house, or one who likes to stick her nose in your flowerpots.

HOW CAN I SET UP AN INDOOR GARDEN?

Let me count the ways

Here are a couple of ways you can set up an indoor garden, especially if you're short on space.

Hanging window garden
If you have a large window with plenty of light, you can hang a series of pots in the window from macramé hangers, little chains, or other dangling devices.

You can also find hanging shelves that you can actually hang in the window and set your plants upon – they are merely a set of shelves hanging on ropes. These make me nervous. I know that if I had one of these, I'd accidentally crash into it and knock down the shelves and overturn all the plants in an instant.

Bay window garden

An easy-peasy choice: Stick all your plants in the bay window, and boom, you're set. I want so much to get a bay window because even a north-facing window would get so much lovely light (though I'd still need to give the full-light plants some grow lights to help them out).

A bay window would also be a good place to keep the hanging shelves that I mentioned now. They're out of reach, so they're less likely to be upended by me whenever I trip over the damn cat.

Kitchen countertop herb garden

Stick some LED grow lights to the undersides of your cabinets, and set your kitchen herbs underneath them, placing them on a raised platform to keep the plants closer to the light.

Windowsill garden

Expand your windowsill with open-backed shelves, if the windowsill is wide enough, and pile on the plants. Or set the plants directly on the windowsill if you have space. However, if you have a cat that methodically knocks things off shelves, make other plans.

Bookshelf garden

Bid a tearful goodbye to a whole shelf of books as you clear them off to make way for plants. Set up track lighting on the underside of the shelf and run the electric cord through a space in the back of the bookcase. Place a waterproof, shallow container on the shelf to protect the rest of the bookshelf from spilled water or soil. Put plants on the shelf. Boom! Plant shelf.

Indoor hydroponic garden

A nice choice for the kitchen countertop is an Aerogarden, or a similar setup with an attached grow light and a hydroponic attachment. One of these plant stations will cost a couple hundred bucks, and you'll need to buy pods and nutrient packets. However, a small, self-contained hydroponic garden is compact, convenient. Light, water, and nutrients are all taken care of for you, and there's no mess. Best of all, hydroponically-grown plants will mature more quickly than soil-based plants – hence their appeal.

Living wall

Hang up a shelf and stick a pretty container with plants on it. Set a grow light to shine on it Boom, vertical garden.

If you want to grow a vertical garden with shelves of garden boxes straight down your wall, this is certainly another possibility.

Countin' flowers on the wall, that don't bother me at all

Grow cart garden

A grow cart is an open-sided shelf on wheels with a grow light or shop lights under each shelf. The plants go on the shelves.

You can buy grow carts that are small as an end-table to carts as big as Godzilla. If you're a dedicated plant fiend, you can get a Godzilla-sized plant cart, load it up with a truckful of seedlings, and roll your plant juggernaut through the dining room to show off. Get out of the way, kids, Mama's moving her damn plants.

Some grow carts have adjustable lights, so you can lower them for tiny seedlings, then raise them as those seedlings grow. If you're a dedicated grower, a good grow cart will be a necessary part of your operation.

You can also get actual side tables or coffee tables with a regular tabletop on top and a place for your plants underneath, complete with grow lights, Just slide the table and plants next to the living-room couch, set your Pepsi on it, and you and the plants can watch old episodes of M*A*S*H together.

Window box garden

Technically, a window box is not an indoor garden because it's outside. But alas, if I had nothing more to do than split taxonomic hairs, I'd have myself bound and shelved in the archives. Anyway, these still count. They're not much good in cold climates during winter, obviously, but they're nice if you need to add a little extra growing space in summer.

As I've mentioned, I am not a design maven, so if you want to see cool indoor gardening setups, do a Google image search, or roam through Pinterest for ideas. There are as many design ideas as you have imagination or resources for.

A nice vertical garden setup for the wall. Image by dieneves.

HYDROPONICS

A fairly short overview

I had originally planned to skip this part because I was leery of discussing something I have no background in. All I knew about hydroponics was they were a system of PVC tubes with holes for the plants. Nutrient-rich water was circulated through the pipes and the plants grew like gangbusters in the nutrient water. I'm a low-maintenance gardener, and this sounded like a lot of work. As a rule, I put a lot of work into avoiding work.

However, all that has changed. Hydroponics is manageable, even for a small household. You can buy compact countertop gardening kits with grow lights and their own hydroponics or aeroponics for the roots. Some have timers to turn the grow lights on and off daily.

Hydroponically-grown plants will mature much more quickly than soil-grown plants, giving you finished crops faster because you can control everything that's going to your plants' roots.

Hydroponics is a method of growing plants in a soil-free solution of nutrient-rich water. No soil is involved, but other growing mediums such as coconut coir or perlite can be used, and the roots grow into a nutrient solution.

Aeroponics is a type of hydroponics in which you grow the plants' roots in a water-tight environment. The nutrient-rich water is sprayed or misted over the roots.

Some aeroponic planters have wi-fi, which allows you to control the device from an app.

(I have to mention that typing that last sentence turned me into a Luddite for a solid minute, but I'm okay now.)

The systems are extremely water-efficient, recycling nearly all of the water and nutrients in their tank. They're also an efficient way to grow food crops. The reason that plants grow so quickly in an aeroponic systems is that the naked roots are exposed to extra oxygen, far more than roots in soil can access.

The plant stations have little lights that blink when you need to add fresh water or nutrients, or notifications that pop up on your phone if you use their app.

You can get big floor models for large plants (tomatoes, peppers) and countertop models for smaller plants (lettuce, herbs, strawberries).

One drawback to these systems is that a power outage could cause your plants to die. Without electricity, the roots aren't misted, and they could eventually dry out as a result.

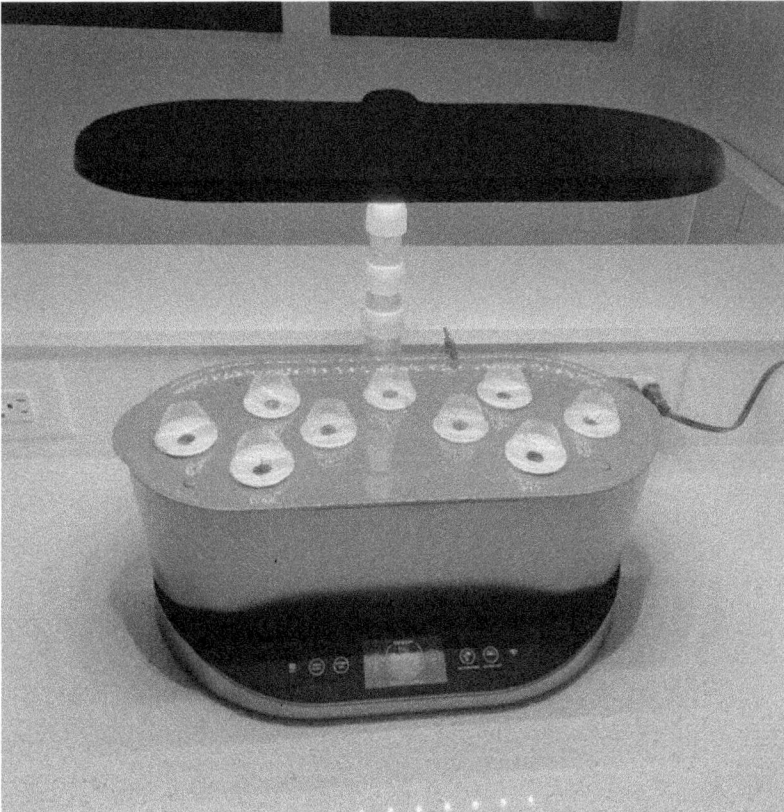

An example of an aeroponics system.

Deep-water culture (DWC) is the simplest way to DIY your hydroponics. Plants sit on top of a tank or container with their roots in the water. You can use a 5-gallon bucket or a plastic storage container, punch a few holes in the lid for the plants, and suspend them in the holes so their roots are immersed. An air pump and air stone will keep the water oxygenated (this is very important, or else the water will go stagnant), a package of hydroponic nutrients, and a pH control kit and a PPM meter to keep the nutrient level in the water at levels to keep your plants happy. Boom, you are now doing hydroponics.

LIGHTING YOUR INDOOR GARDEN

Wherein I really get into the weeds (literally) about the whys and wherefores of lighting.

And speaking of weed, let's take a moment here to appreciate cannabis growers.

No, seriously. If you really want to learn the technical aspects of large- and small-scale horticultural lighting, don't bother with the garden pages on the web. Go straight to the cannabis pages.

These days, when you Google a gardening topic, the search results bring up a lot of copypasta stuffed with SEO keywords and secondhand information gleaned from other internet pages that gleaned their secondhand information from *other* internet pages, and so on, ad infinitum.

But not the cannabis pages. I generally read a lot of science stuff, but let me tell you, when a cannabis grower talks about grow lights, they are serious as a heart attack. The information they give is complex as heck, but once you fight your way through it, as I'm doing at the moment, you start to understand this whole other world a little better.

Photosynthesis – What Do Plants Need?

This is a primer about light and plants and photosynthesis and how it all works!!

Photosynthesis, a process wherein a plant turns sunlight, carbon dioxide, nutrients, and water into sugar or carbohydrates, is how the plant makes the energy it needs to survive.

Some plants need more light, some less, that falls within a certain range of intensity (intensely bright sunlight to dappled sunlight under a shade tree) and duration so the little energy factories inside every cell in every leaf keep cranking out the carbs and sugars that the plant needs to survive.

When a plant is growing, it is diverting energy toward making new cells in roots, stems, and leaves. This is low-energy work. However, when a plant is blossoming or making seeds, almost all the plant's energy is being diverted toward that work, because being able to produce seeds is necessary for the survival of the species.

If the plant isn't getting enough light, it will ration its energy by neglecting its regular processes in order to make sure the flowers and the fruits have everything they need to develop. A few days of low light are survivable. Too much low light, and the plant starts having to use its stored energy to survive. Eventually it runs out of stored energy and dies.

Obviously, we don't want that. Our goal here is to replicate sunlight enough to make our plants grow like crazy so we can eventually eat them for supper.

Sunlight!

Sunlight is very important! Without it we'd be a frozen rock drifting through the endless emptiness of this indifferent universe. With sunlight, life is lollipops, rainbows, and oxygen-producing plants busily working to support the rest of life on earth.

Going back to that rainbow, sunlight can be broken down into a spectrum of light, both visible and invisible, that plants need. And each color in the spectrum causes different photosynthetic processes.

Let's break it down.

How plants respond to different parts of the spectrum
Red light penetrates into the center of a plant's leaf, but not all the way through. It stimulates the production of chlorophyll,

helping the plants absorb energy from sunlight. However, too much red light, with no other kind of light, over a long period of time will cause plants to become spindly and leggy.

Red light is necessary for plant growth and development, stimulating the production of flowers and fruit. Fun fact: Because the sun at different times of day produces different kinds of red light, plants use these changes in red light to tell time and produce flowers at the appropriate season.

Blue light, which has a shorter wavelength, penetrates only into the upper surface of the leaf. This part of the spectrum produces leaf and stem growth.

Green light is not effectively absorbed. It gets reflected off the leaves, which is why most plants are green. It's a minor player on the photosynthetic stage, but still is an important part of the process.

Gamma rays give you superpowers! Or maybe I've been watching too many Marvel movies.

Red and blue lights have long been touted as being "best" for plants, because these are the parts of the light wavelength that leaves absorb for photosynthesis. The plant uses blue light for vegetative growth – for the leaves – while red light is used for flower and fruit production.

However, in the search for efficiency, we've overlooked how other colors also make photosynthesis more effective. Green light, for instance, is more effective than other color wavelengths at penetrating the plant canopy and getting the light to the plants underneath.

This is why full-spectrum light is so valuable, and that's why the pendulum is swinging back toward white, full-spectrum plant lights again.

So your job is to get the right kind of grow lights so your plants can "taste the rainbow."

Artificial Light!

Artificial light lacks intensity. What we consider good lighting is far different from what a plant considers good lighting!

Indoor lighting that seems bright to us looks like near-darkness to a plant. Your average house light doesn't have enough brilliance or intensity to support most plant life.

The regular measurements of lights you see on regular bulbs – lumens, lux, or watts – only indicate the quality of light for humans, but NOT for plants.

The sun's radiation includes much, much more than the visible light that we see. Plants respond to radiation outside of the visible spectrum. UV light affects plants in the same way it affects humans – they can get a plant tan, or they can get scorched. There's also a type of infrared light that induces early flowering in some plants.

Plants don't *need* these other types of light to survive, but they are life-supporting perks.

For obvious reasons, regular indoor lights don't include infrared or UV light, though a few high-quality grow lights will include these for commercial growers.

Is Your Plant Is Getting Too Little/Too Much Light?

It's important to find that happy balance for your plants.

A plant that isn't getting enough light will turn tall and "leggy" – that is, the stems and leaves grow much longer as they stretch toward the light, making the plant tall and skinny. Plants that are not getting enough light start dropping leaves. If you have a variegated plant, the white in the leaves will go away and the leaves turn a solid green. The plant won't bloom. If the situation goes on too long, eventually the plant depletes its energy stores and dies.

Plants can also get too much light, as when you set your houseplants outside for the first time after a long winter indoors. Your plant's leaves will look bleached or scorched, or their tops are browned. If that's the case, move the light away from the plant.

When you get a brand-new lighting setup, break it in by growing some of your less-valuable plants under it and noting how they react to the light. Then you can adjust the light to its best height so it doesn't scorch those trays of tasty microgreens that you've been looking forward to eating.

Grow Light Acronyms and Their Meanings

Swimming Through a Ginormous Bowl of Acronym Soup

Have you ever read *Twenty Thousand Leagues Under the Seas* by Jules Verne, where Captain Nemo and his submarine crew are fighting all those giant squids? That's what writing this chapter has been like.

Human lighting metrics have very little to do with how plants experience the light – so we must use different metrics, which this chapter will cover.

If you aren't really into the technical definitions of various lighting terms, feel free to skip this chapter.

In general, plants achieve efficient photosynthesis with this mix of colors in the grow light spectrum:

About 10 to 20% blue

About 25% green

About 50-65% red/far-red

Some grow lights include UV and infared light, but these have little effect on photosynthesis.

Kelvin

Grow lights are sold with numbers with K behind them. K stands for Kelvin, which is a way to measure color temperature. The higher the Kelvin number, the whiter the light is.

Color temperature and light wavelength are linked. Color temperature describes the color of the light produced by whatever source you're looking at – the overhead light, a grow light, the sun, a flashlight.

Color temperature is measured in Kelvin (K). 1,000K is a warm color temperature (red) while 10,000K is cool (blue).

- Warm light at 3000K help plants produce flowers and fruit (orchids, African violets, cukes, tomatoes).

- Foliage plants do best with 6500K (seedlings, lettuce and leaf crops, herbs, and root crops). 6500K approximates natural sunshine.

Footcandles

Footcandles is a unit of measurement to determine light intensity. One footcandle equals the brightness of one candle a foot away. Direct sunlight can have an intensity of 10,000 footcandles.

Wattage

Wattage is how much electricity the bulb uses – not how much light it puts out. Many low-wattage LED lights are as brilliant as spotlights – they're energy-efficient.

Low light

50-250 footcandles/10-15 watts

A north window or a dark corner

These plants won't require much direct light. In the wild, they would have been understory plants, growing on the forest floor.

Since they don't need as much light, they don't need as much water, too. Most low-light plants are foliage houseplants, like pothos, peace lily, and others.

Medium light

250-1,000 footcandles/15-20 watts

East-facing window or near west-facing window, but out of direct light.

You will need additional light to start seeds in medium light location.

These plants won't dry out quickly.

High light

More than 1,000 footcandle/more than 20 watts

High light is a brightly-lit location in south or southwest-facing window

Can grow seedlings in bright light but they will eventually become leggy without additional light.

Plants will dry out faster in bright light. Check soil frequently.

TRICKIER CONCEPTS

What are CRI and CCT?

CRI is *color rendering index* – how well a light source can reveal an object's true and natural colors, compared to natural light. But CRI also evaluates how closely your grow light approximates visible sunlight.

The maximum possible CRI is 100 – the CRI of sunlight. **A good full-spectrum light for indoor gardening would have a CRI rating above 85, but try to choose a light that is as close to 100 CRI as possible.**

CCT is *correlated color temperature,* which is the color appearance of a white light – how "warm" or "cool" the light is. Blue light is cooler while red light is warmer. In more specific terms, warm light is 2700K; neutral white light is 4000K; and cool white is 5000K. The sun's natural light has a CCT rating of 6500K.

CCT isn't really a good way to compare grow lights because it's based on how humans see the light, which, as you know, is a lot different than how plants experience it.

However, I'm including it here because color temperature can indicate how much blue vs. red light is in the grow lamp's spectrum.

If you want to promote leafy growth, a grow light in the blue range – 5,000 to 7,000K – would work very well. If you want your plants to fruit and flower, a light in the red range – 3,500 to 4,500K – will do the trick.

What is Photosynthetic Active Radiation (PAR)?

This rating refers to light that is valuable for photosynthesis. After all, we are supplying this light to the plant because we want it to photosynthesize enough to *thrive* and live its best life – and to give you big yields in terms of flowers, leaves, and fruit. The PAR rating of a grow light tells you how suitable it will be for your plants' needs.

Let's break down PAR.

When the sun shines on a leaf, part of the light spectrum is absorbed for photosynthesis, while a small percentage of it is reflected from the leaf's surface and not used. The leaf absorbs the wavelengths that it needs – the parts of the color spectrum, from red to violet.

Each plant absorbs different light wavelengths for photosynthesis, depending on their needs. The wavelengths, or type of light, that the leaf absorbs is called PAR.

It's important to note that PAR doesn't measure how much light the plant absorbs – it measures the quality of light. More PAR means the plant is getting more useable light from different parts of the spectrum.

If you're having trouble absorbing all that, it's understandable. Here's a helpful rule of thumb: A good-quality full-spectrum grow light will provide light across the full color spectrum. Thus is a solid choice, especially if all this talk about colors and Kelvin and temperature is confusing the heck out of you. I know it's confusing me right now.

When you look for grow lights online, the array is even more dizzying, especially when you're confronted by a wall of keyword-heavy text from every single grow-light seller on Amazon.

Behold, a sample product description, ripped from several different sources on Amazon.

Grow Lights for Indoor Plants, Full Spectrum Sunlight, 1ft, LED Grow Light Bulbs, T5 Grow Light Strip, LED Plant Grow Light Strips Full Spectrum for Indoor Plants with Auto ON / Off Timer, Grow Light, 80W Tri Head Timing 80 LED 9 Dimmable Levels, Grow Lights for Indoor Plants, Full Spectrum Plant Light for Indoor Plants, 5 Heads Red Blue White Full Spectrum Plant Light with 15-60" Adjustable Tripod Stand, Indoor Grow Lamp with Remote Control and Auto On/ Off Timer Function, Grow Lights for Indoor Plants, 20W Ultra-Thin Invisible Plant Light, Full Spectrum Led Grow Lamp with 144 LEDs, DIY Assembly Grow Light Strip for Indoor Garden Greenhouse Aquarium Hydroponic

Look upon my keywords, ye mighty, and despair.

Hopefully this little guide will pull you out of the sea of keywords and carry you safely to the solid land of knowledge. Read on and learn about the many types of grow lights on the market.

Types of Grow Lights

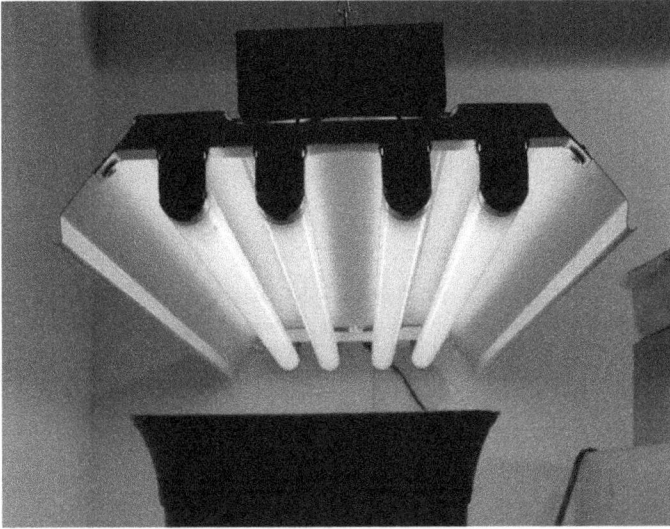

Fluorescent

These are the most common bulb, the one you generally see used in shop lights and in businesses that haven't yet upgraded to LED lights.

Fluorescent lights are very easy to find and set up. If you get a 4-foot metal fluorescent fixture that holds two T8 tubes, hang it right over your plants, and boom, you're in business. These shop lights are great for supplemental lighting (as when you already have a window handy).

Fluorescents are, in general, low-intensity lights – which means the plants should be placed within a few inches of the bulbs for best results. These fluorescents seem to be a general favorite for starting seedlings, as these won't need as much intense light as maturing plants.

What do fluorescent light numbers mean?

Fluorescent lights come in all different sizes. These are the most common.

T5 lights have a diameter of 5/8 of an inch, and have the brightest light while being the most energy-efficient. Some last up to 90,000 hours.

T8 lights have a diameter of 8/8 of an inch – that is, 1 inch.

T12 lights are the big ones with a diameter of 12/8 of an inch, or 1.5 inches, and are the dimmest bulbs. These are being phased out in favor of newer, brighter lights.

T5 tubes need a different fixture (they won't plug into a regular shop light fixture), but they'll give you more rapid and robust plant growth. You can find T5 bulbs with an additional "HO" rating, which means "high output." These are brighter, and much better for all-purpose growing.

Fluorescent grow lights are good for seedlings – choose T5 bulbs with high CCT and CRI ratings. (We've explained what these are in a previous chapter.)

However, it should be noted that T5 high-output lights can put out of a lot of heat, damaging the seedlings. Hang a thermometer at the level of the tops of the plants and monitor it for too-high temperatures.

Compact fluorescent bulbs are great for small spaces. These screw into any ordinary light fixture, like your desk lamp.

Fluorescent lights are more economical, though LEDs outlast them and save more energy. They're also fragile. Whenever I pull those long tubes out of their long boxes, it sets my teeth on edge. Ages ago I accidentally busted one of these lights by turning too quickly and smashing it on a door frame – an experience I have no interest in repeating.

Many fluorescents produce light only in the blue to yellow-green spectrum. The blue lights will produce happy, stocky lettuce, greens, and seedlings. However, you can find full-spectrum fluorescent bulbs that will give your plants the right spectrum for flowering and fruiting. Some indoor growers will put one grow light and one cool (blue) tube into the shop light fixtures, thereby getting the best of both worlds.

The nice thing about fluorescents is that the lighting arrays can be found for sale at a decent price if you look around on online classified websites.

LED Grow Lights

LED stands for **light-emitting diode**. In places outside my quiet plant nook, they cast an unforgivingly brilliant light, especially when I'm outside at night. I'm generally being blinded by LED car headlights, gigantic flashing LED billboards, and LED streetlights that are bright as neutron stars, especially when I go out into my dark backyard to look at the stars but all I can see is that damnable hell-light a full block away, making night into day. I'm going to plant trees to block it, because good grief.

However! When you use LED bulbs in a nice grow light for plants, they are much more pleasant, because they're such a good light for plants. According to research led by Dr. Jim Tidwell at Kentucky State University, LED grow lights, seem to perform best in terms of the total plants grown and crops produced, outranking fluorescent, halides, and induction lights.

LEDs are energy-efficient, lasting five times longer than conventional lights while using half the electricity. LEDs also have better CCT and CRI ratings and don't get hot like other lights.

If you have a large growing operation, high-end greenhouse-quality grow lights can cost over a thousand bucks. However, very good, greenhouse-quality lights can be found for $80, and even less if you have a smaller operation.

Again, you can't use an LED light straight out of housewares. Seek out some proper LED *grow lights*, which are brighter and produce light in the spectrums that allow your plants to prosper.

LED panel lights, an example of which is shown above, work very well with larger groups of plants. They put out very little heat, so you can use big groups of these lights in larger growing operations without burning the house down. And they're also good for a smaller operation as well.

Panel lights can be hung from the ceiling or attached on a shelf to shine down on the seedlings or plants below it. (Before hanging panel lights, check to find out how close this light should be to your plants/seedlings, so you don't install it and then have to readjust the height later.)

Generally, a cheap LED grow light will cover an area of 2x2 or 3x3 feet.

Incandescent

These are the classic light bulbs. If somebody gets an idea, an incandescent light bulb appears over their head.

These lights aren't recommended for plants, because they're energy inefficient, create lots of heat, don't put out a lot of light, and are on the red end of the spectrum, which will cause plants to get leggy unless you add in supplemental lights.

So, these are not recommended for grow lights.

HID Grow Lights

High-intensity discharge lights – HIDs – used to be the go-to lights for large indoor plantings before LEDs showed up, because they put out a lot of light over a wide area. HID light is very good at penetrating *into* the canopy of large plants like lemon bushes, and of course marijuana. As a result, more interior leaves receive the light they need to stay healthy.

Also, with HID lights, you can run a 400-, 600-, or even a 1,000-watt light using regular household current. (The 1,000-watt light would cover an area of up to 8x8 feet.)

However, these lights are expensive, use a lot of electricity (surprise surprise), require special light fixtures, and can generate a lot of heat in a very short amount of time.

This is because HID lights produce full-spectrum light – which includes infrared light, which heats all surfaces it touches. Most plants prefer a room temperature of 70 to 75 degrees, so with

HID lights, you also have to run fans and air conditioners to help regulate the temperature – which also affects the humidity of the room!

Yeah, it's a lot.

LED lights have been replacing HIDs, because they put out comparable amounts of light while using a lot less electricity and generating very little heat. LEDs also result in shorter, stockier plants, because red-spectrum light (which the HID lights put out) tends to make plants stretch out, creating longer stems and leaves.

Narrow-Spectrum LED, "Blurple" Lights

These Narrow-Spectrum LED lights are commonly known as "blurple" lights because they give off mainly red or blue PAR wavelengths, with a tiny bit of the other colors in the spectrum.

Blurple is the color of the combined red and blue lights on your grow light. Together, these colors cause plants to form more compact growth.

However! It's important to note that using only two light frequencies could end up limiting plant health.

If that's the case, then why are so many grow lights available in only blurple?

The old LED lights used to be expensive, both in terms of cost and efficiency, so manufacturers designed these plant lights that left out the "non-essential" light frequencies in order to save energy.

However, the older studies didn't assess how the different kinds of light frequencies worked to complement each other, or how the full light spectrum was better for the plant's overall health.

These days, blurple lights are being left behind for full-spectrum lights. These give the plants a wider range of colors, and the white light is more pleasant than the weird blurple light. I was always frustrated by blurple lights because I could never enjoy the full beauty of my plants or their flowers. It's also harder to tell if something is wrong with your plants if you can't see their real color.

My pretty orchids and other plants
all in a gorgeous(?) monochrome of blurple

Full-Spectrum Lights

Technically, a grow light isn't truly full-spectrum the way the sun is. After all, it's probably not the best idea to have a light that emits infrared or ultraviolet rays in your house.

Full-spectrum bulbs offer a broad range of hues, blending reds, blues, and greens, mimicking natural sunlight. Plants and their flowers look so much prettier under a full spectrum light, with bright and clear colors.

You can also choose full-spectrum white lights that lean more toward one side of the spectrum or the other. If you want a cooler look for your home, choose a bulb that leans toward the blue side, one rated between 5000-5500K, which is also good for vegetative growth. If you want a warmer light temperature, choose a bulb that leans toward the red part of the spectrum, about 2700-3500K. These are also better for flowering and fruiting.

It can be tricky to figure out which white LEDs are actually full-spectrum. However, grow light packages will have images of light spectra on the side or bottom. Try to get one that shows as much of the full spectrum as possible.

High-intensity, full-spectrum LED lights will deliver a very brilliant light indoors. These lights can deliver 2,000 footcandles to a plant that's 30 inches away from it – an intensity that is somewhat like full sunlight.

And the high-intensity light will also penetrate the plant's canopy, bringing light to the leaves underneath. Fluorescent lights can't deliver this kind of reach, which is why fluorescents work best on short plants under 12 inches tall. With taller plants, you'll get a plant with dark green upper leaves while the lower leaves become puny.

High-intensity lights are popular with marijuana growers because these LEDs can deliver good-quality light through the top leaves that reach the lower leaves, even on plants that are five to six feet tall.

SEEDS

Propagation is the science – and art – of plant reproduction. If you're going to start your plants from seeds, this chapter is for you.

Be sure to have enough room for your seedlings before you start – and make sure the area is warm and has good air circulation (easy to fix if you get a little cheap fan from the dollar store).

This book will discuss sprouts later on. Even though there's a whole lot of propagation going on in the sprout-growing process, I put all the information about them in the next chapter with the vegetable crop profiles. The germination processes for sprouts are markedly different than the ones I'm discussing in this chapter for other crop plants.

How to Do a Germination Test

To raise seedlings, you need to give them water, soil, and warmth. A heat lamp is great, or a heat mat under the seedling trays if your room is especially cool. Once the seeds sprout, move them off the mat under some lights. As the seedlings grow, thin them out (you can eat them as you do if they're leaf crops)

If you're worried that your seed might not be viable, here's a germination test you can run at the same time you're planting your seeds. Take about five extra seeds and lay them on a paper towel and fold the towel over them, then moisten the paper towel so it's wet but not dripping. Put the towel inside a sealed sandwich bag and keep it near to where the seeds are germinating. (However, if the seed flat is in direct sun, move the plastic bag into a shaded location.)

If you get impatient, wondering how the seeds in your pots are faring, you can hold this plastic bag to the light and see how well the seeds are progressing, or you can open up the bag and peek at the seeds.

Protip: If you have a bunch of seeds left over after you've planted your spring garden, combine those that have similar germination times, then plant the leftover seeds in a single tray all together.

WORK OF THE SEASON

Starting Seeds in Containers

*Swiped and amended from my Easy-Growing Garden book, **If You're a Tomato I'll Ketchup With You**.*

Starting plants from seed has always been a fun activity. From browsing the colorful seed catalogs, to seeing the new shoots breaking the soil, to enjoying the harvest of these once tiny plants – it's amazing how you can get five hundred pounds of zucchini from a tiny seed.

If you grow your plants from seed, it's best to start them in late winter on a windowsill or in a cold frame. At any rate, many seeds need a soil temperature of at least 60 degrees to germinate, though some prefer warmer temperatures up to 80 degrees.

You can start some of your seeds under lights as early as February. Then, when the weather is mild enough, transplant the young plants to their designated container outside, using sheets or mulch protect the plants against surprise frosts and freezes.

On your calendar, count six to eight weeks back from your last frost date, and that's the date you sow your seeds. (Protip: Keep a gardening calendar and notebook where you write down things like sowing dates, the dates you see frost, etc. Then you can use this information next winter when you're planning for the upcoming planting year.)

Next, line up your planting containers. Seedling containers can be made with all kinds of found containers. Used food containers work well, as well as yogurt containers and toilet paper tubes with the bottom folded up.

Milk jugs cut in half make great seedling containers. Cut off the bottom of the milk jug, punch drainage holes in it, put in the potting soil, then add in the seeds and cover with soil. Put the top of the milk jug back to hold the moisture in as the seedlings germinate. Rotisserie chicken containers and clear salad containers also are great for starting seedlings.

Whether you use old egg cartons, Solo cups, or flowerpots, wash them with hot water, soap, and a dash of bleach. Cleaning up the trays/flowerpots will clean up any diseases that might be harbored there – diseases that could affect young seedlings.

Be sure that, whatever you use, your planter has plenty of drainage holes! This is not negotiable!

How to Plant Seeds

When sowing seeds, it's best to use a light seeding mix that is high in vermiculite. This kind of seeding mix is lighter and easier for newly-germinated seedlings to poke their little green heads through. However, a regular "soilless" potting mix works fine in a pinch.

When I ran the city greenhouse, I always started my seedlings in trays. I'd pour a scoop or so of moistened seeding mix into the tray and tamp it down – the guys at work made a really nice tamp for me out of a piece of wood that fit the length of the tray with a handle on it, so I'd spread out the soil, flatten it, and sprinkle in the seeds.

The late George Ferbert, who owned greenhouses in St. Joseph, Missouri, for years and years, showed me a little trick when seeding flats: He'd add a little bit of sugar to the seeds before he sowed them. The sugar shows up against the black dirt so you can see where the seeds land, so you can broadcast them more evenly around the surface of the soil. Lobelia seeds are tinier than even the sugar crystals. When I added a little sugar to the cup of seeds to "see where they hit," the sugar crystals stick out of the Lobelia seeds like boulders in sand.

At any rate, when you mix the tiny seeds with a half-teaspoon of sugar, that helps the seeds scatter out, keeps them from clumping, and you can see where the seeds and sugar fall into the soil. You will have to keep mixing the sugar and seeds as you sow, because the two substances will not stay evenly mixed. Fine sand also works with tiny seeds. You can use this method whether you're sowing the seeds scattershot or in neat rows.

If you prefer to plant seeds in rows, take a #2 pencil, dab the point lightly into water and wipe it off, then touch the pencil to the seed to pick it up. Then you can use the pencil as your dibble – that is, use the pencil to make the hole and plant the seeds.

Once the seeds are sown, shake ¼ or ½ of soil over the top of the seeds, depending on the depth the seed packet recommends, gently tamp the soil down, and water. I used a super-fine spray head on my watering wand, taking care not to let the water puddle in the tray. If you can find a watering can with a super-fine spray head on it, you're set.

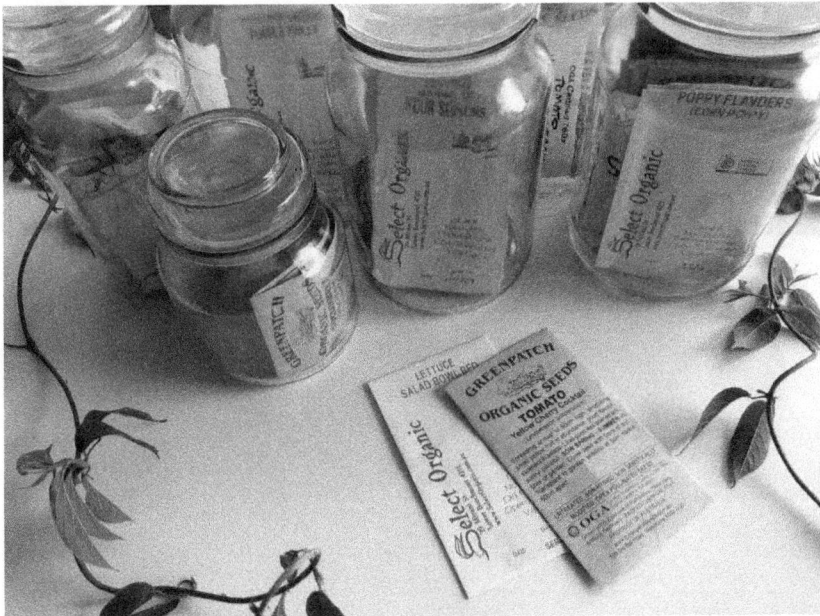

For those of you with a small-scale operation, seeding is a little less involved. Fill your pots, cups, etc. with potting mix, leaving about a half-inch to an inch at the top. Poke two or three seeds into the middle, about a quarter-inch deep, and cover them. (You're planting two seeds in case one doesn't sprout.) When they get bigger, pinch out the wimpier seedling and let the larger one grow.

Gently pack the soil in around the seeds, because seed-to-soil contact is important for good germination rates.

Sprinkle water on the soil and keep the soil moist. Dry soil will kill the seedlings, and constantly wet soil will rot them.

One way to keep the soil from drying out is to cover the trays or pots with plastic wrap. If you use plastic wrap, don't leave the trays in direct sunlight. One time I had the soil covered this way on one of my flats. I came in from one of my jobs and realized that it had been sitting in the sun all afternoon. I ran over and lifted up the plastic wrap – and steam puffed out. Those seeds were roasted!

Seeds will germinate more effectively if you have a heat mat under the cups or trays. This will warm the soil with dependable heat, allowing the seedlings to germinate and grow out more quickly. be sure to get a thermostat with the mats so you can adjust the temperature so you don't end up cooking your seeds.

Once the seeds germinate, be sure to remove the plastic wrap, and have a small fan to keep the air circulating around them. Seedlings are susceptible to a disease called "damping off" which is encouraged by poor air circulation – more about which you can find in the next chapter.

COMMON PESTS AND DISEASES

Insect pests and diseases are common plant problems, and with this, as with anything, the best defense is a good offense. Actively check your plants every two weeks for signs of any little bugs. If you see either one, isolate the affected plants while you try to kill off the pests, and keep them isolated until you're able to get rid of the pests or throw the badly infected plants away.

The best defense is a good offense. (Or is it the other way around?) Here are a few simple tips to stop pest infestations before they start.

Ways to Keep Pests and Diseases Out

1) Any time you bring home a new plant, or bring one in from outdoors, keep it separate from the others for a about six weeks, and check it for pests once a week. Plant stowaways are the most common infectors of household plant collections.

2) Monitor your plants. Pick them up and gently rub the leaves between your fingers. Check the newest leaves on the plant, as these are the most tender leaves – and the most vulnerable for hungry pests. If you see something odd, rub it off with your finger (if they're scale insects, you'll need to gently scrape them off with your fingernail).

3) Give your plants a spa day every month. Stick them in the sink and spray them with water, cleaning off their leaves and stems. This is a good way to find pests and squish them and spray them off the plant before they can get a foothold.

4) Invest in some yellow trap cards. You can get these off eBay or Etsy for cheap, and you can post them up around your plants to catch flying insects. These are especially helpful if you've had problems with fungus gnats or whiteflies in the past. Also, when you see a new pest show up on the cards, you can immediately give all your plants a spa day and stop infestations while they're still easily stoppable.

5) Get rid of any dead or dying leaves and other plant wastes. Don't let these accumulate. Keep the plant area tidy. These could give pest insects a place to hide.

6) If you notice a plant looking odd, or different from its usual state, or looking a little under the weather, whisk it away to quarantine and see what the matter is. Give it a little extra attention. Sometimes a plant simply feels a little mopey and needs a little TLC. Sometimes the plant has something eating it – literally, like a pest or a disease. Either way, separate the plant from the others until the issue is resolved.

7) Most of these tiny pests can be wiped off with a Q-tip dipped in rubbing alcohol. Make sure the alcohol doesn't affect the surface of the leaf too badly, as some plants are sensitive to it. The alcohol kills the insects pretty effectively. Don't use too much, of course, as it can hurt your plant.

Mealybugs

These insects afflict indoor and outdoor plants. Mealybugs are generally wingless, whitish, oval bugs about 3 millimeters long, and look like tiny bits of waxy fluff. Some have long white "tails". Newly hatched mealybugs, called nymphs, are flat, oval, and yellow. Once females mature, they stick themselves to the plant, cover themselves with a powdery wax layer that repels water (and insecticides), and suck plant juices.

Mealybugs feed by sticking their threadlike mouthparts – the proboscis – into the plant, inject a little of their saliva into the plant to liquefy the cells in that area, then they suck out the plant juices. Naturally, when a bunch of mealybugs do this, the plant becomes stunted, or wilts, or dies back.

Mealybugs multiply easily and can be hard to kill, and by sheer numbers can overwhelm the plant. They also excrete honeydew, a sugary substance, and in a plant with lots of mealybugs, the honeydew they leave behind is infected by sooty molds, turning the plant a sooty black color.

Male mealybugs resemble whiteflies or tiny white gnats when mature. They have wings and can fly around. However, females are wingless, and must be transported to new host plants to infect them. They can crawl short distances, but more often, the nymphs can be blown by the wind to a new plant to infect, or can be picked up on the feet of birds as stowaways. Most often, an infected plant is set down next to an uninfected plant, leaves touching, and the mealybug nymphs gallop across the gap like wild horses.

When they first arrive on a new plant, mealybugs tend to wedge themselves into the crevices, generally in those tiny spaces where a leaf joins the plant stem. But then a female makes an ovisac, which looks like a waxy bit of cotton, and lays some eggs in it. Once that first batch of eggs hatch, that's when the infestation starts. Other females join in the egg-laying spree, and then you have a mealybug crisis on your hands.

Some mealybug species, such as the Madeira mealybug, can have up to five or six generations every year. Imagine multiplying so fast that you could live on the same plant as your great-great-great-great-great-grandchildren in the space of a year! Females can lay, on average, 300 to 400 eggs in their lifetime. Sometimes they can lay eggs that immediately hatch.

For all these reasons – the rapid-fire egg laying, the many generations in a single year, the relative waterproof-ness of the insects and the wooly egg sacks – it's a challenge to stop a mealybug infestation.

Outdoors, predators such as green lacewing larvae and ladybugs can attack mealybugs and bring their numbers down (except when ants protect the mealybugs, farming them for their honeydew). But indoors, without the help of predator insects, control is even more of a challenge.

Use several points of attacks in getting rid of infestations. Isolate the afflicted plants. Spray neem oil on the places where the mealybugs are congregating, concentrating on the places where you see the mealybugs. You can also spray them with insecticidal soap or pyrethrin.

Also, dip a cotton swab into rubbing alcohol and touch it to each mealybug you see. The rubbing alcohol will eat through the waxy coating that protects the insect, drying it out and killing it.

But if you spray them, you should also squish them. Mealybugs can develop resistance to different insecticides – but they'll *never* develop resistance against being squished. Check the bottoms of the leaves and stems for mealybugs and their nymphs and squish them wherever you see them. Use a toothpick to squish any mealybugs that have packed themselves into the crevices of your leaves and any other tight places where your fingers can't reach.

I recommend squishing or otherwise wiping out any insect pests when possible if it doesn't make you feel ill. This work is time consuming, especially if you must keep coming back again and again, as when each new batch of eggs hatches. But when you squish them, then spray, you have a better chance of beating down the infestation.

Whiteflies

These insects look like tiny white gnats, no more than one or two millimeters long, and they generally feed on the undersides of plant leaves. These are not flies, however – they're more closely related to mealybugs and aphids, so their life cycles are similar – as are their control methods.

Despite their name, some forms of whiteflies are actually black or grey, but they generally have something of a flour-y look, as if they were dusted with flour. There are hundreds of different species of whiteflies, afflicting many kinds of plants.

You can tell a plant is badly infected when you touch the plant and a swarm of tiny whiteflies rise into the air from the leaves.

Like its annoying distant cousins, the mealybugs and aphids, whiteflies also excrete honeydew to get ants to protect them from predators.

Whiteflies lay eggs, and the larvae emerge, looking like mealybug nymphs. They crawl around until they find a place to settle down and feed, whereupon they stop crawling and attach themselves to the plant by its mouthparts (a proboscis). After a time, it changes inside its own skin, creating something like a pupa, and once its metamorphosis is complete, out pops the adult whitefly, complete with wings.

Like the mealybug and other members of the Hemiptera family, these insects can cause sooty mold to attack the plants they've dropped honeydew on.

Also, while the whiteflies are feeding on the plants, they inject saliva into the plant cells to break down the cell innards so they can easily suck them up through the little straw that is their proboscis. Naturally this is toxic to plants, and they feed in such large numbers that a plant can easily succumb.

Whiteflies can also transmit diseases and harmful viruses from plant to plant, such as tomato yellow leaf-curl begomovirus, which is a devastating viral disease.

When a plant is infected with whiteflies, immediately separate it from the others and wash it off with water with a little soap added. Gently rub the leaf bottoms with the soapy water to rub off whitefly larvae or strip them of their protective waxy coating. Rinse by spraying the plant with water to further knock off any larvae, let the plant dry, then apply neem oil, insecticidal soap, or pyrethrins.

Repeat this regimen once a week. Put up yellow trap cards around your plants to catch any flying whiteflies as well.

You can use insecticides, but whiteflies quickly develop resistance to these, so be sure to include the mechanical means of control – the soapy water scrub and the yellow trap cards – for best results. Remove any yellowing or dying leaves and seal them in airtight bags so whiteflies don't hatch on these and repopulate your plants.

You can even vacuum the air around your plants if the infestation is that bad – or if you feel particularly frustrated. Start your vacuum, shake the plant, and suck the flies right out of the air. Take care not to vacuum up your plant, of course. You might hold your plant with one hand and hold the vacuum nozzle with the other and try to keep them far enough apart to avoid damaging the plant, as you shake the plant and brush off the bottoms of the leaves. Dispose of the vacuum bag away from your plants, sealing up the dust so those little jerks can't escape.

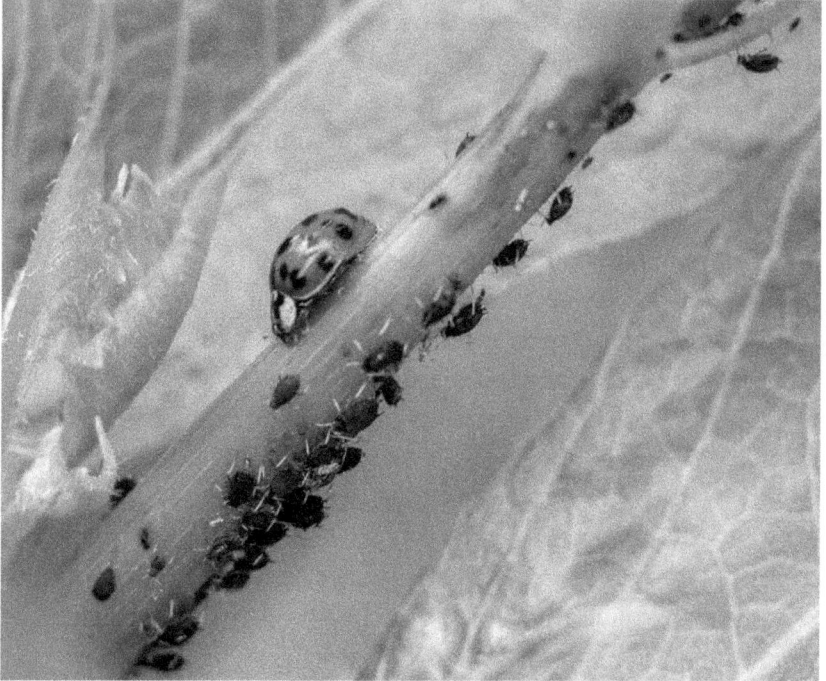

A hungry ladybug going aphid hunting. © *Friedrich Haag /* <u>*Wikimedia*</u> <u>*Commons*</u>

Aphids

These are tiny, soft-bodied insects (also in the Hemiptera family) that are often green but can also be pink, orange, brown, or yellow. Most are smooth-bodied, some have little bits of cotton or a waxy coat on them. Some are winged. They're all a nuisance.

Like their cousins, they will drink out of the plant with their proboscis, leaving yellow and misshapen leaves, stunted growth, and deformed buds. Aphids reproduce through laying eggs and live birth, and they multiply like the devil.

As with the others, use multiple means of eradiation: squish them, spray them off the plant with water, wipe them down with the Q-tip dipped in rubbing alcohol, and spray them with insecticidal soap, neem oil extract, or pyrethrins. Quarantine the plant and keep repeating these treatments until they're gone.

Fungus gnat (not actual size)

Fungus gnats

These are annoying little flies that are either flying directly at your eyes, or they're running across the soil of your plants, flitting their wings.

The adult fungus gnats aren't as much of a problem as their larvae are, however. These live under the soil, eating your plant roots. If you're trying to start cuttings in soil that the fungus gnat has laid eggs in, you'll uproot a cutting to see why it's taking so long to grow, only to see a couple of fungus gnat larvae, which look like tiny white worms, wriggling in the bottom of the cutting that they've been eating their way through.

Get some sticky yellow trap cards and post them around your plants to catch the adults. Flypaper is cheaper and more readily available.

The easiest way to stop the larvae is to pick up some BT mosquito dunks from the store. Be sure that the active ingredient in these is the *Bacillus thuringiensis* (BT), a type of bacteria that targets fly larvae and caterpillars and kills them. Break up one of the dunks and let it float in your watering can, then water the plants with it. You can leave the dunk in there as long as you like. This water will carry the BT into the soil and slowly kill off the larvae. After about two weeks, you should be gnat-free.

Carnivorous plants like sundew or pitcher plants will eat fungus gnats, though it takes some degree of skill to raise them. (I've managed to kill two sundew plants within weeks of each other, and I'm allegedly a professional.) But it's pretty cool to see fungus gnats stuck on a sundew's leaves.

Scale

Many of the more destructive insects (at least here in the Midwestern United States) come from the Hemiptera order – mealybugs, whiteflies, and scale insects. Scale insects are insidious because they're harder to spot. I've seen little spots on my plant and don't even think twice – until I notice that the spot has magically moved to a different location, and has been joined by smaller spots.

Rule of thumb (not for scale insects but others as well): If you notice honeydew on your plant's leaves – a sticky, shiny, sugary spot – then you have one of these insects lurking on your plant. Give your plant a bath with slightly soapy water, splashing and rubbing the leaves to find the insect culprits, and squishing the heck out of them. Look on the undersides of leaves, on the leaf stems, and in the nooks and crannies where the leaves meet the stems.

Spider mites

Not actually spiders but they're distantly related.

These are very small, very hard to see, and generally one doesn't realize there's a problem until they notice that the leaves look as if they've faded, and they have very tiny yellow or bronze stipples all over them. Sometimes there are tiny webs on the plants.

Spider mites like try conditions and hate water, so an occasional bath, which includes spraying and gently rubbing the leaves clean is a relief to the plant and a curse to the spider mites. Neem oil might work best against these, as the oil closes up their spiracles (the little breathing things in their bodies).

Cats

I seem to really have it out for cats in this book for some reason.

Hopefully your cat is well-behaved and doesn't sit on your plants, or eat them, or use them as a litter box. Some pieces of double-sided tape left on the table around your plants, where the cat might walk, might help to discourage Mr. Attitude. I don't know if leaving cucumbers out to frighten your cat is still a viral video thing, but if leaving a cucumber near my plants is going to keep my cat from sticking his face in them, I would do it.

Your typical insouciant cat

You can also grow a pot of grass for your cat to eat (*Poa* spp., not marijuana), or a pot of catnip, so they have their very own plant to sit on.

Yelling "Get down, kitty!" at them from across the room never works. A Nerf gun with soft foam bullets might be more effective, but only if you have good aim. Otherwise the cat sits in the sink, staring at you like "Seriously?" as soft foam bits go zinging past him.

You can also put aluminum foil on the edge of your table where your cat jumps up. I saw a TikTok last night of a cat that hopped up to a counter and landed on the aluminum foil. Its crinkle caused the cat to ricochet himself across the room to escape it. When it comes to cats, you have to find your amusement when you can.

Damping-Off Disease and Mold

Swiped from <u>Big Yields, Little Pots: Container Gardening for the Creative Gardener</u>

Back when I was a city horticulturist, I had a bout of damping-off disease in my greenhouse, and it was a mess. Damping-off is a fungal disease that causes newly-planted seedlings to keel over at soil level and melt away. It spreads out in a circle, as most funguses do (as with "fairy rings," which are circles of mushrooms on the forest floor), killing off seedlings as it spreads outward.

I hadn't experienced damping-off disease before, since I kept the soil on the dry side in the greenhouse, which the fungus didn't like.

That all changed after a whole week of cloudy, cold weather. My trays of seedlings, watered on a Sunday, would not dry out for the rest of the week. The sun refused to come out, and I couldn't turn on the fans to pull the air through for very long because it was too cold outside. Humidity was high. All the conditions were right for the fungus to strike.

Then the disease got into the snapdragons I'd planted and started knocking them out everywhere. I got on the phone and called everyone I could think of for help. Then I took their advice, and it worked.

The best defense is a good offense. Keep a fan always running to keep the air circulating. You should feel the air moving through the whole room, but you don't have to turn it up so high that it blows the mice out from under the floor. Space the plants out to let air circulate between them. The fungus likes high humidity and temperatures about 70 degrees. The fan keeps the humidity and temperature lower.

This will break your heart, but get rid of everything that's been infected by the fungus. Dump out the soil and the plants with them, and take the waste outside so spores won't reinfect the plants. As soon as you see the seedlings keel over, and you know that it's not due to being underwatered, out they go.

Mold, in small amounts, is actually a regular part of plant life. It's only when the mold colonizes and gets out of control that it becomes a problem. Some microgreens, like sunflowers, are especially susceptible to mold.

Fortunately, there's an easy fix. Give the tray a moderately heavy watering from the top – this will wash the excess mold and spores out of the soil. Let the soil drain for a little bit, then place the tray under lights and turn a fan on them.

This usually does the trick. If it doesn't, go in with a spoon and dig out the moldy parts. Then add fresh potting medium to fill in those spaces, and you're good.

Hydrogen peroxide is sometimes touted as a way to kill mold and funguses, and it is an option, but when used in the wrong dilution, can kill your plants. The heavy top-watering is a more natural way.

Mold and fungus spores are always present. Sanitizing your trays and pots will knock out the worst offenders. Then keep good airflow and lights on your plants to keep them from getting a foothold.

The Importance of Good Air Circulation

As we saw above, air circulation is extremely important when it comes to growing inside. Outdoors, there's always a breeze nosing around, sometimes a gale. Inside, the air is still, which can lead to problems down the road with fungus and mold and whatnot.

You don't even need a huge fan. Well, okay, if you have a large operation, you will. For a small operation, a regular-sized oscillating fan will work, or a cheap box fan turned on low. Even a clip fan will do the trick (and a clip fan can be moved to different places, as needed).

Bonus #1: A breeze helps the young seedlings and the growing plants develop sturdy stems. When you start running a fan on your seedlings, it's crazy how quickly they adapt and straighten up. This helps with older plants too, but it's best to catch 'em when they're young.

Bonus #2: If you're growing plants that need pollinated, such as peppers, eggplants, tomatoes, or strawberries, the fan also scatters those pollen grains for better pollination (and we'll have more about pollination for certain indoor plants later in the book).

The Importance of Taking Notes

What's a way to get consistent, excellent results in growing indoor plants? By writing about your plants and growing schedule in your gardening journal.

A gardening journal isn't for outdoor plants. It also works great for your indoor plants as well, and especially food plants.

Write journal entries as you garden. When you start a crop, write down what kind of growing media you used, how many seeds you planted in how many flats, what kinds of plants you started, how much water you give the plants, how much weight you placed on top of the soil while waiting for the seeds to germinate, harvest weight, and many other things.

Of course, you can also write daily entries about your life and about your plants' lives. But writing things like this down helps you see what works and what needs to be improved in your plantings. The more data you gather about your plants, the more you learn about growing them. You can keep lists that track of all the variables that have gone into your gardening, cross-reference this information with other info that might help your friends and you to do better.

Green side up, y'all

GROWING PLANTS INDOORS

Leafs, Sprouts, Roots, and Other Crops!

At last! What we came here for in the first place: The plants!!

SIDE NOTE: I have a whole slew of plants in my Big Yields, Little Pots container gardening book that can also be grown indoors under lights if you have the space for them. I'll provide entries for some of those plants here with the information you need to grow them, but this book will have additional information specifically geared toward indoor growth.

Smaller crops, such as microgreens and shoots, are often grown in greenhouse trays.

Use potting medium instead of soil to grow these crops. A good potting soil has no actual soil in it. Actual soil brings in diseases and pests from outside, which can proliferate in a pot because there's no soil food web of small creatures and microorganisms to keep pathogens in check, as there would be outside.

An inert potting medium that uses coco coir, perlite, or peat moss is best for indoor gardening. Use a light, fluffy soil blend that drains well. Seeds sprout more easily when they can pop up, and roots are happier when they're digging through fluffy soil.

Coconut coir is more absorbent than peat moss (the old standby) and more earth-friendly, as it uses up discarded coconut hulls that would ordinarily have been thrown away, while peat moss is actual sphagnum peat dug up from bogs in Canada. Recycle and reuse, folks!

Growing new celery in a flowerpot. Pic by Milada Vigerova

How to Grow Leftover Kitchen Scraps

Gardening, as I mentioned earlier, can be a wonderful way to reuse, recycle, and renew. This chapter is no exception: You can regrow different leafy vegetables from your own kitchen, including romaine lettuce, cabbage, bok choy, celery, carrot greens, turnips, radishes, beets, herbs, and more. Even pineapple!

Leafy vegetables such as lettuce, cabbage, celery can be regrown from the bottom of the stalks. Cut off the leaves so an inch of the plant's base remains. Set the base in a shallow bowl, add enough water to cover the base, and give it full sun. Replace the water every couple of days. Eventually new leaves start growing from the centers, and roots will form.

Carrot tops can be used a lot like parsley (they are both in the Apiaceae family) and can be added to salads or soups.

Once they do, you can replant the base in a pretty little container, covering the roots with soilless potting mix while leaving the tops exposed. Or you can simply let it keep growing in the shallow water. This won't give you a whole new lettuce head, but you will have leaves to add to salads.

Cut and come-again harvesting is when you clip what part of the plant you need, then let everything grow back. With this method, you can grab a couple of leaves every week and then you have another batch ready to go in a week or two. Most lettuces (except head lettuces) are good for this, as well as any greens and herbs.

Harvest the smaller leaves on your lettuces for the best flavor. Eventually the lettuce will get spindly and blueish, and you can send it to the compost bin.

Root vegetables such as carrots, radishes, and beets can also be grown this way. You will not get any new carrots or beets out of them (sorry), but you'll get the leafy greens, which are good for salads, soups, or sautéing.

When you buy fresh herbs at the store, or cut them from the garden, save the stems and set them in water, with a couple of leaf nodes underwater, to root and plant so you can grow your own herbs.

Green onions can be grown on your countertop. Place the bulbs in one or two inches of water, changing the water daily, and trim them from the top whenever you need them. Keep them in less than 2 inches of water so they don't get icky. Water is best for growing them – green onions don't like being planted in soil for some reason.

Mung beans. Photo by Anan 2523

Sprouts

Plant type and name – Multiple types
Growing methods – In jars and containers; no soil
Light – Keep away from direct light
Water – Rinse them on the first two days
Temp – Room temperature or cooler
Fertilizer – Not necessary

Sprouts are an easy and quick way to raise food in a tiny space. They're tasty, economical, healthy, and it's kind of fun to raise them and try different types. The kids always love raising these.

I honestly did not realize there was such a variety of sprouts that you could grow the heck out of in your kitchen. Beans, peas, alfalfa, soy, chia, popcorn, barley, lentil, wheat, kale, turnips, sunflower, sesame, pumpkin, quinoa, amaranth, cabbage, radish, mung bean, lentil, chickpea, and rye – and more!

Health-food stores are good sources for seeds for sprouting, as well as mail-order sources.

You can also use some organic, pesticide-free, inoculant-free seeds – actual seeds meant for sowing in your garden. However, avoid dried food seeds (like beans, corn, or peas). These make disappointing sprouts, and their germination rate is low.

Choose a container made of plastic, china, enamel, or unglazed pottery that has a lid you can close. No metal or wooden containers. Chances are that you have several containers around the kitchen that will fit the bill.

A large-mouthed container is easy to work with. A Mason jar is a popular choice because it's easy to strain out the old water daily. Any Tupperware or Rubbermaid container with a lid works great.

But you can also use any such container for sprouts. If you bought spinach or salad in one of those large clamshell containers, rinse it out and use that. To-go containers! Soup take-out containers from the Chinese restaurant! An old potato salad container! It's all good.

You can also get round, stackable plastic bowls with drainage holes around the edges for sprouts. Lay the seeds down in each layer, stack them, then water from the top. The water trickles down to keep the sprouts moist and doesn't collect. Pour out the water in the bottom bowl and water with fresh. It smells a bit funky when you sprout beans, but nice when you're doing other sprouts.

The size of the container you use for sprouts will depend on how many seeds you plan to sprout, and how big these seeds are. Naturally, you'll need a larger container for peas and beans, and a smaller container for chia seeds.

Other things you might need when you're growing sprouts include measuring cups and teaspoons, paper towels, and a large wire mesh strainer.

You can get sprouting lids for your Mason jars. This is simply a specialized lid that costs a few bucks that hold the sprouts in while you're pouring out the bad water. Or you could use a cheesecloth or wire-mesh cover to strain the seeds the old-fashioned way.

Protip: Start small. Find out which sprouting methods work best for you. Find out what sprouts taste the best to you. Then ramp up to larger batches.

What Sprouts Need (and What They Don't)

First, some science!

Germination begins when a seed absorbs water, and the seed begins to transform from a quiescent dormant thing into a living being with roots and leaves. Inside the seed coat, once the water is absorbed, chemical changes begin, and the seed starts putting out carbon dioxide and other gases. It even generates a little heat from these new processes.

If you leave your seeds in water to sprout for too long, the waste products from these seeds will accumulate in the water, turning them sour and spoiling them. Rinsing the seeds twice a day flushes out the waste products and leaves happy, tasty sprouts.

(Side note: "Twice a day" can be any time during the day … it's not going to make the seeds fail or explode if you can't take care of them at specific times. Rinse them before you go to work and again after you get home – or when you wake up and before you go to sleep. They ain't particular.)

How to Sprout Seeds

Again, and I say this a lot, start small. As the old commercial said, "A little dab'll do ya." One ounce of peas, mung beans, and similarly-sized seeds generally will equal one cup of sprouts, while ¼ cup of these seeds will give you about two cups of finished sprouts.

First, put the seeds into a strainer and rinse them well in cool water to clean them off. Be sure to rinse them VERY well, because poorly-washed seeds could harbor pathogens. (I'm not saying this is something that happens a lot – this is merely a precaution.) Then put the washed seeds into your Mason jar, pouring in warm water to cover them. If you have a cup of beans in there, put three or four cups of water over them. Instead of putting the lid back on, securely tie a piece of cheesecloth over the top, and let them sit 8 hours or overnight.

(It's important to note that larger seeds, like peas and beans, will swell up as they absorb water. If you put too many in, they could fill the jar up!)

The next morning, the seeds will have expanded nicely. Some seeds will be floating at the top. These seeds are sterile and won't germinate, so get rid of them, as they will simply rot. Pour the rest of the seeds into the strainer and rinse them in cool water. Pick out seeds that are cracked or broken.

After this, simply use the mesh or cheesecloth covering on your Mason jar to strain the water out of the jar. Rinse the sprouts a couple of times, check and remove floating bits or bad seeds, then set the jar upside down for a few minutes so it can drain completely. Keep the jar out of sun or direct light. Do this rinsing and draining two or three times a day, inverting the jar each time to keep the water from collecting.

After the first few days, if you're sprouting legumes (that is, any members of the pea family), swirl them around inside the jar when the seed coats start coming off, to knock them off so the seeds can properly sprout.

Keep the sprouts between 50 and 70 degrees.

When are the sprouts finished? When their little white roots emerge. Let them grow a little bit, tasting them as they grow, and soon you'll figure out what stage of "done-ness" tastes the best to you.

Once your sprouts are big enough, give them a final rinse and check for bad bits. Put them into your strainer, a handful at a time, rinse them gently with a spray of water, and drain well. Take out any seeds that haven't sprouted, along with anything mushy or brown. Remove seed hulls if they're large and bulky.

(Be sure to rinse them well!)

Roll your sprouts around on some paper towels and let them lie for about an hour. The seal the finished sprouts tightly in a plastic bag or a storage container lined with a paper towel, and keep them in the fridge. If they start to wilt in the fridge, rinse them in the strainer, roll them again in the paper towel to get the excess water off, then put them back in the fridge.

Use sprouts in your soups, sandwiches, salad, or stir-fry. Unused sprouts in the fridge should be good for seven days. Throw them out into the compost pile if they start turning brown.

Pea shoots (and peas). Pic by T Caesar.

Shoots

Pea/Sunflower/Popcorn Shoots
Growing methods – In containers or pots with soil
Light – 8 hours sun/10-12 hours light
Water – Evenly moist, not too wet
Temp – Cool to warmish
Fertilizer – Organic only, a week before harvest

Shoots are sprouts taken to the next level. You grow them in a pot and cut off the young shoots and eat them.

Pea shoots are started in trays or pots in the potting medium as if you're starting regular peas. The night before you plant them, soak the seeds overnight in clean water to sprout them. (Soak them for no longer than 24 hours.) The next day, sow them densely in the tray so they're almost touching, use a second tray to press them into the soil, then cover with a thin layer of potting soil.

Cover the tray with plastic wrap to keep the seeds from drying out. Keep the tray out of direct light at this time.

Once the seeds start germinating, remove the plastic wrap and set the tray in a full-sun window where the peas can get 8 hours of light, or under plant lights for 10-12 hours of light. Mist the soil when it starts getting dry.

Start clipping the shoots when they're about six to eight inches tall, cutting them off about an inch above the soil. You can clip and eat as you go, or you can clip the whole tray and store the extra sprouts in the fridge for up to 7 days.

Pea shoots, as well as other vegetable shoots, can resprout if you cut the shoots above the bottom set of leaves. The second flush won't be as impressive, but they're still tasty.

Microgreens

Growing methods – Seedling trays with soil or special pads/mats

Light – Full sun 8 hours/ artificial light 12 hour

Water – Moist but not wet

Temp – 18-22 C, 64-70 F

Humidity – 50% or lower

Fertilizer – Sometimes if it needs a boost

Microgreens are grown until their true leaves emerge, and then you clip them above the soil line to harvest. These make cool additions to salads and are also used as edible garnishes. Microgreens are also loaded with nutrients such as Vitamin C, E, and K, as well as lutein and beta-carotene.

Microgreens will give you more bang for your buck because they're quick to start and grow, which is super-nice. Seeds for lettuce and other greens germinate quickly, and these guys are salad-ready within 10 to 25 days of seeding. Once the microgreens

74

germinate, you have about 7 to 11 days before the true leaves emerge (that's when you should harvest).

You can use regular garden seeds for microgreens. Since you'll be eating these seedlings soon after they shed their seed coat, use organic seeds.

What you need:
Seeds
A container (with drainage holes!)
Sterile potting mix, or growing mats
Scissors or a sharp knife, for harvesting
A place that gets bright, direct light for about 10-12 hours daily, or a grow light set about 10 inches above the flat.

A light soil is best. In fact, you don't even need much soil in your trays. A centimeter to about a half-inch of soil is all your seedlings need, since they're going to be growing here for only about 10 days.

Many microgreens growers use cotton pads or coconut coir pads instead of potting medium. These are special pads that fit into a tray, and seeds are sown and grown directly on top of them. Mats are available in hemp, jute, coco, or cotton. Pads gives you a cleaner work area. Microgreens work best in a more sterile environment, anyway.

Regular garden trays work fine but it can sometimes be a challenge harvesting microgreens due to their higher sides, making it hard for you to get your scissors or clippers into some parts of the tray. Heavy-duty shallow trays are available for microgrowers. You'll save money on grow media, harvesting the greens is easier, the trays don't break if you look at them cross-eyed, and you can carry them with one hand when they've been watered.

But you can grow microgreens in any container you please, especially if you're starting out. Grow them in a flower pot or in old takeout containers if you like. The plants don't care!

They also grow best in lower humidity. Ideal humidity is 50%. High humidity can cause mold outbreaks in the sprouts. Have an oscillating fan running over the microgreens to keep the air moving and help keep down instances of damping-off disease (discussed in a previous chapter) and other ailments.

Growing microgreens – Microgreens are a very short lifecycle crop. You won't need fertilizer, because they already have all the nutrients they need from the seed they sprouted from.

Some seeds, such as peas and beans, will need to be soaked before planting, and you'll need a colander to rinse the seeds before you plant them.

Sow the seeds thickly, so they're almost touching. These plants can be grown very densely. Cover the seeds with about a quarter-inch of potting mix. Some growers don't cover the seeds at all, to keep them clean so you don't get surprise dirt grains in your microgreens salad. Keep them moist by misting them daily, or water them from the bottom.

Grow them in darkness for the first day or two by covering them. You could even stack the trays on top of each other if you're growing larger seeds. This weight keeps the germinating seeds in close contact with the soil and helps the seed coat to fall off. Once the young shoots are growing, bring them into the light.

After about two weeks, the microgreens should be ready to harvest. Baby salad greens generally take three to four weeks. The last 24 hours when the true leaves are emerging is when the sprouts have a growth spurt.

Harvesting – Microgreens are generally ready to harvest in 11 days, but you can harvest them as soon as their true leaves emerge after their seed leaves.

I keep talking about seed leaves and true leaves, and here's a little primer if it's been a while since you had Biology in high school. The seed leaves, or cotyledons, are the embryotic leaves that are formed inside the seed, and they're first leaves to unfurl when the seedling pops out of the seed.

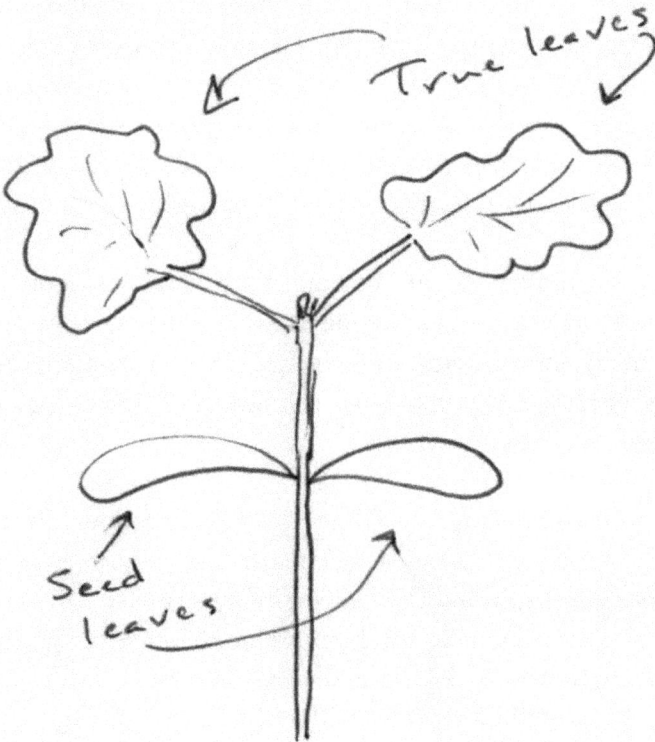

Cotyledons (seed leaves) vs. true leaves.

Fun fact: All flowering plants are divided into two groups. Plants with one cotyledon are called monocots (monocotyledons), and they include grasses, pine trees, orchids, palm trees, and lilies. Plants with two cotyledons are called dicots (dicotyledons) and include oak trees, tomatoes, radishes, and pretty much all the plants listed in this book. This has been your botany lesson for today.

Cut and eat the microgreens within a few days after the true leaves emerge, because they'll start to get bitter. Don't water them the day or two before you harvest.

When it's time to harvest, clip them off above the soil and put the microgreens in a big bowl. Fill it with water briefly to soak them, dry them in a salad spinner, and roll them a paper towel. Then put a dry paper towel into a big ziplock bag and put the greens in there. Poke a few holes in the bag because the greens will give off gasses that will affect their freshness, then store them in the fridge.

You can also cut and eat microgreens as you go, clipping a quarter-tray of greens at a time as a sandwich/salad topper.

The nice thing about these is that you can prep another tray of seeds and have them newly germinated and ready to go when the first tray is ready to harvest.

Troubleshooting – Microgreens won't need fertilizer because there's a lot of nutrition packed into the seed to give the baby plants a good start in life. That's why these are so full of nutrition. If you really must give the plants a small boost of nutrients, give them a light dose of liquid seaweed.

If the seedlings grow tall and skinny, or they're leaning toward the light source, bring your light source closer to the seedlings.

Sunflower microgreens. Photo by Natthapat Aphichayananthanakul.

Growing microgreens commercially – Some folks grow microgreens for local restaurants or sell them at farmers' markets and have made a nice little side gig at this.

If you decide to get into the microgreens business, start small and see how much mileage you get out of it. It's best to make sure you enjoy this work before you drop a thousand bucks on materials. Once you're doing well, then scale up.

There are also hydroponic setups that use water to grow microgreens. Instead of growing seeds on a mat or in soil, you use a simple silicon mesh mat, which is reusable. This would save on materials and waste. Growing microgreens with hydroponics gives you yields comparable to soil-grown microgreens, but you also get a slightly quicker harvesting date.

Whatever method you use, cut off the roots of your finished product if you're growing microgreens commercially. First, because if you sell them with roots on, you're technically growing sprouts, not microgreens, and sprouts are more tightly regulated because root hairs can harbor pathogens can. Heaven help you if the health department catches you selling sprouts without controls and documentation!

Leafy Vegetables

Leaf vegetables (lettuce, spinach, etc.)
Growing methods – In containers and soil
Light – Full sun 8 hrs/Artificial light 12-14 hrs
Water – Keep moist but not soggy
Temp – Cool, 10-15 C, 55-60 F
Fertilizer – Use a granular, 10-20-20 fertilizer. Also use an organic nitrogen (fish emulsion) up to a week before harvest.

An amazing array of lettuce, kale, chard, and other salad greens can be found in heirloom seed catalogs in all kinds of different sizes, shapes, colors, and forms.

Lettuce needs about 12 to 14 hours of bright light daily. A south-facing window is great if the light is not blocked by trees or roof overhangs. Even with a south window, you'll need supplemental lighting. Some panel lights would work, or two 40-watt cool white fluorescent lights that are 6 to 12 inches over the lettuce for 12 to 16 hours a day.

The best types of lettuce to grow inside are loose-leaf lettuce, because they take less space than head lettuce. However, there are some adorable small-head lettuces that will fit the confines of your pots.

Sow lettuce seeds ¼ inch deep in a tray or container with drainage holes. If the room is cold, keep the soil warm with a heat lamp. Thin them out as they grow, or let them grow to 3 inches tall and start selectively harvesting little lettuces for your salads, giving the remaining lettuces more and more room. Do your best to not disturb the roots of the remaining lettuces! If the plants flop over, pile a little soil around their base to stabilize them.

Lettuce can be harvested at 4 weeks or earlier. You can use the "cut and come again" method where you cut the leaves off above the growing parts and let new leaves grow out.

If you're growing spinach, good indoor varieties include Renegade and Butterfly.

Keep leaf crops on the cool side, 55 to 65 degrees. These are cool-season crops, so when they start getting leggy or send up a flower stalk, the leaves will turn bitter and not very tasty.

Great choices for baby greens include lettuce, arugula, basil, chard, and spinach.

Time to thin the lettuce! Pic by heesulee81

Root Vegetables

Radishes

Growing methods – In deep containers in fluffy, light potting mix

Light – 8 hours full sun/12-16 hours grow light

Water – Keep soil moist but not soggy

Temp – Keep cool to avoid bolting

Fertilizer – NPK of 10-20-20

Radishes are a good choice for indoor gardens because you can squeeze a bunch of them into a container. Radishes take about three to five weeks to mature – so when you finish up one pot, you can have another pot of them growing. You can also eat the greens – waste not, want not.

Daikon radishes is not a good choice for indoor container growing, since some varieties can get up to 15 inches long and several inches wide. But if by some miracle you can find a short variety, then go crazy.

Radishes will need to have lots of light (12 to 16 hours of grow light daily) and a decent-sized container to grow in, one that's at least six inches deep.

Radishes grow best in cool weather. If they get too hot, they'll bolt – send up flowers – and turn wooden and bitter.

All root vegetables require a soil that's light and floofy, a soil that's super-easy for a root to grow through and expand in. There can't be any grit because they don't like bumping into grit. A soil that's mostly peat moss or coco coir is a good, light choice. Note that coir and peat alone will not have any nutrients, so you'll need to mix a granular, slow-release fertilizer into it.

Radish seeds are tiny. Sprinkle them over the soil, then sift soil over them until they're well-covered. Water them in, and they'll start germinating in about a week. Thin as needed. Give radishes enough room to plump out without crashing into their neighbors, so thin with an eye toward giving each plant enough elbow room to prosper.

Mammoth Red or Strainer are good, medium-sized radishes for container growing, as well as Cherry Belle, Icicle, Scarlet Globe, Champion, Comet, Sparkler, and White Icicle.

Carrots

Growing methods – In wide containers at least 12 inches deep (a five-gallon bucket is ideal) or deeper, with fluffy, light potting mix
Light – 8 hours full sun/12-16 hours grow light
Water – Moist or slightly on the dry side
Temp – Keep cool to avoid bolting
Fertilizer – NPK of 10-20-20

Again, keep the temperatures cool where you grow carrots, as they'll bolt and the roots will turn bitter.

Grow carrots in a container that's at least 12 to 15 inches deep, with drainage holes. Fill this container with light, fluffy soil to within an inch of the top so your carrots have plenty of legroom.

Poke planting holes into the soil that are about a half-inch deep, spacing them a half-inch apart and from the edge of the container, drop three carrot seeds into each hole, cover them with a ¼ inch of soil, and water them. Keep them watered and warm as the baby seedlings come up.

Some folks cover the pot with plastic to keep the moisture and warmth in – but keep the pot away from the sun so you don't accidentally bake the seeds.

Seedlings should appear in 6 to 10 days, though some might take up to 21 days. This will vary by variety – check the back of the seed packet for specific germination times.

When seedlings are about three inches tall, fertilize them every other week with something low in nitrogen but higher in P and K. A granular or liquid fertilizer with 10-20-20 (that is, 10% nitrogen, 20% phosphorus, and 20% potassium) and trace minerals will work well.

As the carrots grow, keep thinning out the smallest seedlings until each carrot plant has at least two inches of space around it. The baby carrots are perfectly edible once you clean them off – you can enjoy both leaves and root.

Carrots need full sunlight for 6 to 8 hours a day, or supplemental lighting such as grow lights for 10 to 12 hours a day.

If the carrot's shoulders are sticking out of the ground, they'll turn green in the sunlight. Fix this by putting enough soil over the tops of these carrots until they're covered.

Carrots are ready to harvest when they turn orange (or red, or yellow, or even purple, depending on what variety you're growing). Harvest carrots when they're young. If they get old, they'll turn woody and the roots will crack.

If you want more carrots over a longer harvest time, start a second pot two weeks after the first – then a third pot two weeks after the second – then a fourth pot two weeks after the third – ad infinitum.

Choose a shorter carrot variety to grow in your pots, such as Oxheart (this is a chubby, wide carrot, so give it space), Round, Parmex, or Rondo.

Chantaney is a "red-cored" carrot in the classic carrot shape – broad, fat shoulders and a tapered tip – and grows only 4 to 5 inches long.

Other good container varieties include Danvers Half Long, Short 'n' Sweet, Tiny Sweet, Scarlet Nantes, Gold Nugget, Little Finger, Baby Spike, Thumbelina, Parisienne, Paris Market, Romeo, and Caracas.

Protip: Use your carrot tops in garnish and salads. Carrots are a member of the parsley family, so use them in ways similar to parsley. When you thin your carrots, you can eat the baby carrots, but you can also use those greens. Keep them in a bucket of water the way you'd do with cut flowers. Put a handful of carrot greens in your smoothie. Or sauté the greens lightly with garlic, red pepper, salt, and olive oil.

(Be sure to remove the woody stems on the carrot tops before preparing them for supper.)

How about herb sauce? Make a lemon carrot top pesto with carrot tops, spinach, olive oil, parmesan, pumpkin seeds, lemon juice, garlic cloves, and salt and pepper. Use a cup of tops and spinach, then add the other ingredients to taste. Drop them in a blender and pulse them until you get a delicious sauce for fish and other dishes.

Beets and Swiss Chard

Growing methods – In wide containers at least 12 inches deep (a five-gallon bucket is ideal) or deeper, with fluffy, light potting mix
Light – 8 hours full sun/12-16 hours grow light
Water – Moist or slightly on the dry side
Temp – Keep cool to avoid bolting
Fertilizer – One with an NPK of 10-20-20
Time to harvest – 50 days to 90-95 days

As a rule, growing beets in pots yields different results compared to beets in soil. Don't expect large beets like you can grow in the garden – you'll get small bulbs, if any! I recommend simply growing beets for the greens. If you do manage to get good-tasting beet roots, count it as a bonus.

Be sure the pots are at least 12 inches deep, or deeper. Five-gallon buckets with drainage holes drilled into the bottom are great choices for root crops. Even though the roots you eat will grow only a couple of inches wide, their feeder roots want to go deep into the soil, and once those roots hit the bottom of the pot, they stop growing. Containers will dry out faster and overheat in the sun – but growing them under an LED grow light indoors can keep them cool.

Like carrots, beets will need to be directly sown into the soil, at least ¼ inch deep, and the seeds gently watered in. You can plant them an inch apart, then thin them out until they're at least three or four inches apart.

Seed packets will often say 50 days from germination until harvest, but sometimes when you're growing in containers, you're going to find that this is a damn lie. Sometimes it takes 90 to 95 days to develop a beet.

Choose a fertilizer that is low in nitrogen if you're trying for beetroots. Give them the maximum acceptable dose of fertilizer THOUGH NO MORE THAN WHAT IS RECOMMENDED ON THE PACKAGE, thank you – because root containers are heavy feeders.

Mix bonemeal into the growing soil for phosphorus, and do this every year with each new crop of beets.

Growing beets and chard as greens

Beet greens and Swiss chard are fantastic on their own, and if you simply focus on growing them as greens, you will meet with better results. You can eat the leaves right out of the garden if you like, or pick them and cook them as greens with red pepper and bacon.

If you grow beets as greens, like their botanical cousin, Swiss chard, you can use a container that's not as deep, and give them a fertilizer higher in nitrogen, as this will give you large, tender leaves. Again, as with other plants, you can use them as "cut-and-come-again" crops for longer yields. After a while, the greens will turn bitter, so compost them and start a new crop.

Other Vegetables

Some plants are not worth growing inside if you're looking for a way to save money. Yes, you can grow potatoes indoors, but that is a lot of soil and labor to use when you can simply go to the store and get 10 pounds of potatoes for five bucks.

On the other hand, if you're a die-hard gardener and you want to grow some of the more hard-to-find potatoes, like fingerlings, or if you're simply a fanatic who WANTS to grow potatoes indoors, then by all means, rock on.

Peas

Growing methods – In containers with soil
Light – 8 to 10 hours daily
Water – Let dry out slightly between waterings
Temp – 15-21 C 60-70 F
Pollination – Self-pollinated
Fertilizer – A light fertilizer is fine

Peas are not normally the first thing that pops to mind when one thinks of indoor gardening, but if you have a long shelf with shop lights or LED lighting overhead, along with a small trellis of some sort to help these guys sit up and not flop all over each other, and a place to grow them where they can stay cool – then you're in business.

Granted, you're not going to make a five-course meal out of these plantings. But you'll have lots of pea shoots to cook, and fresh peas to snack on for a little while.

Sow the peas directly into 4- or 6-inch pots, between a half-inch to an inch deep – one pea per pot. The peas will need about 8 to 10 hours of light daily. If you have adjustable grow lights, hang the lights over the pots when the seedlings pop out of the soil, then raise the light as the peas grow (as you don't want a bunch of pea tendrils wrapping themselves around your grow light). Keep them a couple inches over the peas as they grow.

Window light also is good if you have a southern exposure that will give 8 hours of full sun daily. be sure the peas don't get hot. They grow and bear best in cool conditions.

Once they start sprouting tendrils, start them on a trellis, tying the pea vines to it with twist ties. (Save these from your bread bags.) Any wire grid is fine, or wooden dowels, or strings.

Peas won't need pollinators – they're self-pollinating!

Small, manageable varieties of heirloom peas to grow inside include Sugar Snap, Little Marvel, Tom Thumb (grows only 8 to 9 inches tall), Early Frosty, Norli, Oregon Sugar Pod, Patio Pride, Avola, Märta (a yellow snow pea), Canoe, Capucijner (a blue-purple heirloom pea from the 1500s), Hurst Green Shaft, Desiree Dwarf Blauwschokkers (a dark purple), Shiraz, and Carouby de Maussane.

The beauty part is that, since many of the above varieties are heirloom seeds, you'll get the usual green peas, but some of these peas are yellow or purple. You'll also get pretty white, pink, and magenta blossoms to liven up your home.

Little bumblebee doing all the work for you. Photo by Markus E

Plants That Need Pollination

For the next plants, we need to talk about POLLINATION!

Because I'm pretty sure that none of you plan to keep a little hive of honeybees in your house – which means you're going to have to handle pollination yourself.

Pollination is not too hard if you have a little time and a Q-tip, or a little soft paintbrush. You'll need to transfer pollen from a different flower to stigma of the flower you're pollinating, for every flower, if you want to grow something tasty after you've put this much effort already into growing plants indoors!

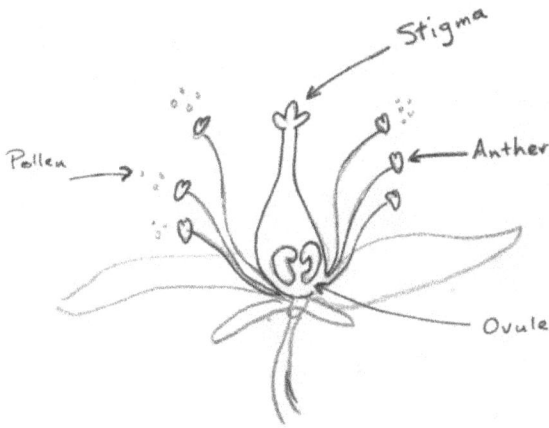

Parts of a flower…because your high school biology class was probably a couple of years ago

Gather a bit of pollen from the anthers (shown in the diagram) using a soft paintbrush, a Q-tip, or a toothpick, and put that pollen on the stigma on another flower. Then repeat repeat repeat on every flower you see. If you have multiple plants, use the pollen from one plant to pollinate another, for best results.

Strawberries require a little more effort as every single one of the stigmas will need to be pollinated so you don't get misshapen fruit. More about that in the "Strawberries" section.

Peppers, Eggplants, and Tomatoes

I'm combining these three since they're in the Solanaceae family (aka the nightshade family). One useful thing to remember about plant families (and this goes for insect families too) is that they'll share many of the same needs as others in their family, and are often susceptible to similar insect pests and diseases.

91

Peppers and eggplants (as well as tomatoes) enjoy warmth and lots of light. A large grow light suspended about 10 inches over them, one that can be raised as they grow, is ideal. They (along with tomatoes) are heavy feeders, so plant them in a well-draining potting soil and add a water-soluble fertilizer such as Osmocote to their soil, and water them with an additional dose of fertilizer every two weeks.

Pinch back the tops a couple of times while they're still young to encourage them to bush out – so they're growing out instead of up.

Have a fan blowing on them to keep the air circulating, as these three plants are susceptible to fungal diseases such as powdery mildew.

Once they start flowering, the fan will help circulate the pollen. These guys are wind-pollinated, so the pollen will be very light and fine and easily drifts around on any breeze.

To help with pollination, flick the flowers a little bit to help scatter the pollen, or give the plants a little shake now and then to get the pollen out in the air.

I also have used a toothpick to move pollen from the anthers to the stigma to make damn sure they've been pollinated, because I want my tomatoes, people.

Additional Tomato Tips

Choose determinant tomatoes – indeterminate tomatoes keep growing and growing. They'll take over your whole house if you let them.

Though I can see where a tomato-filled house could be a win for some of you tomato maniacs … until it comes time to clean up after them. Choose your wins carefully.

Start tomatoes in small pots, then after they grow their second set of true leaves, transplant them into a bigger pot, such as a five-gallon bucket with holes drilled in the bottom, or a ten-gallon pot. Tomatoes, and many plants with similar fibrous root systems, like being transplanted. (Those with a long tap root, such as parsley and carrots, hate being transplanted.)

Use a garden tower to prop them up in order to try and avoid tomato calamity in the form of gigantic plants falling over. Or do the sensible thing and keep cutting back your suckers.

Add 10-20-20 fertilizer granules to the soil and an additional tablespoon once a month, water about every 3-4 days once the top inch of the soil is dry.

They'll need 10-12 hours of light daily. If you have an especially large tomato plant with lots of interior leaves and stems, invest in a full-spectrum grow light with more green in the spectrum. The green light penetrates more deeply into the canopy to reach the interior leaves and stems so they can photosynthesize, too.

If you have a tomato plant that you're training up next to a window, provide supplemental bright light in the form of a panel pointing at the plant's side and the wall, or several gooseneck lamps with full-spectrum LED lights aimed at the foliage.

Zucchini

They need full-spectrum lights to keep them happy, 12-16 hours of light.

These plants need heat – like tomatoes, they luxuriate in heat.

Give them fresh potting soil in a 10-gallon pot, or larger, and mix. They're heavy feeders, so add fertilizer to the soil and then water them with an all-purpose fertilizer.

Start by choosing a more compact variety, since the large, sprawling varieties don't do well in containers. Zucchini varieties with "Bush" or "Patio" in the description are good picks, as well as varieties like Black Magic, Spacemiser, Cube of Butter, Hybrid Jackpot, Burpees Golden Zucchini, Bush Baby, Raven, Gold Rush, Silver Bush, Classic, Black Beauty, or Cueball.

Put a well-drained potting medium into a 5-gallon pot, or larger, and stir in an appropriate amount of slow-release granular fertilizer (to determine what an appropriate amount is, always read and follow label instructions).

Zucchini like a moist soil that doesn't quite dry out, but they shouldn't be left standing in water for an extended period of time or else they get root rot.

Plant seeds 1 inch deep, two seeds per 5-gallon pot. Sprouts should appear anywhere between 7 to 14 days. If it takes longer, plug in a space heater nearby on low because your plant is too chilly. Maybe give it a sweater as well, Zucchinis love the heat.

Shine a grow light on your plant for 10-14 hours per day, placing it about 6 inches away from the top of the plant.

Zucchinis, being zucchinis, will keep vining, so set up a support for them, such as a trellis. When the vines start crawling out of bounds, snip off the growing tip to stop the creep.

A cross-section of a female zucchini flower. Note the mini-zucchini at the bottom of the flower.

A cross-section of a male zucchini flower

Zucchini pollination

About two months after germination, you should start seeing your first flowers.

Zucchini have both male and female flowers. The female flowers have a zucchini-shaped bulge directly under the flower base. The male flowers have only a skinny stem. To pollinate, use a Q-tip or small paintbrush to transfer pollen from the male flower to the stigma in the middle of the female flower. Or you can pick a whole male flower with lots of pollen in the middle, pluck off the petals, then dab the pollen directly on all the female stigmas. Repeat as new flowers open! You should see the young fruit start to swell within 36 hours of pollination.

Strawberries

When you're looking for strawberry varieties for your indoor garden, choose everbearing or day-neutral strawberries, because these will put out runners and new baby plants over time, and they bear for a long time in the right conditions. Junebearing plants will put out a lot of strawberries at once, then they croak at the end of the season.

Try to get live plants instead of seeds, whether they be potted or bare-root. Seeds take longer to get started, and at least with plants, you know exactly what you're getting. Bare-root plants will take a little longer to reach maturity but still take less time than seeds.

Strawberry roots need a very-well drained potting soil, because they fail in low-oxygen situations, such as a soggy soil or a very heavy soil. They will need a lot of water, but at the same time they don't like being overwatered, and often develop crown rot or root rot as a result.

While you're growing your plants, maintain them by removing runners, allow no more than three crowns per plant, and remove small flowers on the flower stalks if you have more than three to a stem. This will give you larger flowers.

Strawberry pollination

Here's why pollinators are especially important to strawberries. Most flowers have one ovary where a single seed forms. To pollinate it, you transfer a little pollen from the anther to the style – boom, done. Not with strawberry flowers. A strawberry flower can have *up to 500 ovaries*. On the full-grown fruit, these ovaries turn into the little strawberry seeds all over the fruit – biologists call them achemes.

Every one of these little achemes needs a bit of pollen. Photo by Gernot.

Every one of those achemes need to be fully pollinatesd. Strawberry flowers can pollinate themselves, but pollinator insects provide much better coverage, pollinating up to 91% of the achemes.

When a group of achemes are not pollinated, you end up with a deformed berry with a clusters of little green seeds, usually at the bottom of the strawberry, that doesn't taste very good, or a little green seedy nubbin. However, when the strawberry is fully pollinated, you get a big ol' happy red berry that looks gorgeous and tastes sweet.

(Fun fact: Some studies have indicated that achemes might contribute to the antioxidant compounds in the strawberry.)

Pollinated strawberry fruits will take their sweet time in developing. Just hang in there.

Strawberries need lots of light and water (but don't water the leaves as they will burn easily). In low light their leaves will die off.

Beans

When growing beans indoors, stick with bush beans. These are a better bet than pole beans, which can grow between 6 to 10 feet tall – and it might be tricky and expensive to put grow lights over all that area. Bush beans don't need trellises or vine supports, they're much more compact than a 10-foot-tall vining behemoth, and they're easier to harvest.

Each bean plant will need 1- to 5-gallon pots with well-drained potting medium. Plant a couple of beans about an inch deep and water them in; these should germinate in 7 to 9 days. After a week, thin out the plants to one per pot.

Keep the beans between 70 and 80 degrees for best results. Set your grow light about six inches over the foliage as it grows.

Bean plants should start flowering after a month. They don't need to be pollinated! Still, you can help them along by shaking the bean plants to help scatter the pollen. Running a fan on them also helps. You will get tiny baby beans, and finally full-grown beans about 50 to 70 days after germination, ready to harvest. Snip the beans off the plants, and take care not to damage it.

Be sure to give your beans a little more water once flowers appear. And watch out for insect pests on beans, such as spider mites or aphids.

Meyer lemons and other small citrus trees

Growing lemon trees from lemon seeds might not give you viable fruiting trees, or even fruit, as lemon trees don't grow true from seed – that is, the tree that grows from the lemon seed will be genetically different than the parent tree. You might get good lemons, or you might get weird little lemons, or you might not get a fruiting tree, or you might get a grapefruit, of all things!

It's like the gardening lottery: Maybe you'll get a winning ticket in the form of good fruit, or not – but whatever happens, you always win this lottery with a pretty plant.

Plant your lemon or citrus tree in a large pot.

In summer, move the tree outside, if possible. Start it out in the shade, gradually moving it into the sun to acclimate it to the light. If summer is hot, double-pot it to keep the soil from getting too hot. Double-pot means to put the smaller pot inside a larger pot, then put some kind of insulating material between the pots. This will help keep the roots cool, and keep the trees from dropping their blossoms.

While your potted tree is outdoors, give it a thick mulch of lawn clippings (organic) in summer, on top of the soil. The mulch will insulate the soil and roots against the sun, hold in water, and keep it from evaporating, and keep topping off the mulch. The lemon tree will need to be watered more often while outside.

Before you bring the tree back indoors, spray it off with the garden hose and check for insect pests such as mealybugs, scale insects, aphids, and treat them by blasting them with the garden hose, spraying them with soapy water or neem oil, and squishing any pests with your fingers. Clean up the tree, trimming dead branches and leaves, which also helps you find insect pests. Keep after the pests after you bring the tree indoors, because that's when a lot of them pop up.

Spider mites are hard to see, but they show up as very fine grit, like large dust, on the bottoms of leaves, and there will be small webs. Drag the tree to the shower and spray the heck out of it, and rub off what webs you can. Put a humidifier nearby as spider mites hate humidity, but keep cleaning leaves and sliding your fingers over them to get the mites off the leaves. Wash your hands well before working with other plants so you don't spread the pests.

In winter, set it next to a huge bright window. For best results, supplement the natural light with a grow light on a timer, turning it on in the early morning, then again in the evening for a few hours each time.

Put something washable under your citrus trees because they will drop sticky sap on the floor.

Fertilize your tree with something specifically made for citrus trees, since they have specific, specialized needs.

Pollination

Meyer lemon trees are self-pollinating, for the most part, but they could use your assistance when they're indoors. You can shake the tree and turn a small fan on them to circulate the air. But you'll need to get a small paintbrush or Q-tip and play the part of a bee. Go from one open flower to another on the tree, dusting pollen on each blossom. If the flowers are ready to be pollinated, the stigma will be sticky and catch the pollen you're spreading. Repeat this work every three days to increase your chances of success.

Harvesting

Lemons take a long time to grow to harvest! You have to wait for the fruit completely ripen before picking it – which can take from six months to a year for indoor trees. Growing the tree outdoors will ripen the lemons more quickly. They will be ripe when they're slightly soft to the touch and bright yellow.

Pic by **NatureFriend**

GROW YOUR OWN HERB GARDEN

Herbs are the perfect way to bring fragrances into your kitchen. I cannot walk past a rosemary plant, or a lavender, or sage, or thyme, without ruffling the leaves and breathing in their fragrance. I generally pluck a leaf or two to carry in my pocket and enjoy its fragrance for a little bit longer.

You can take cuttings from established herbs to get new herbs. Basil, mint, cilantro, thyme, parsley, lemon balm, oregano, and sage are all pretty easy to sprout from cuttings. Cut two or three inches of stem from the plant, clip off the lower leaves, and stick it in a couple of inches of water for a few weeks until roots form. Pop the baby herb into a pot with soilless potting mix. Keep the soil moist and grow your baby herbling in full sun.

You can also start them from seed, or simply pick up full-grown plants from your local nursery. I'm an impatient gal and generally prefer potted herbs for that reason alone. A potted herb plant costs about the same as a container of fresh-cut herbs from the store, and they last longer.

When picking a potted herb plant, avoid specimens with brown spots on the leaves, big empty spaces in the plant, wilting, or a general hangdog look. Look for cheerful, full, green plants with lots of stems. Check it for pests or diseases.

Also, choose plants that are not blooming. Blooming plants divert a lot of energy to produce flowers and fruits. If you buy a non-blooming plant, all their energy will go toward developing roots when you repot them.

Finally, remember that not every herb grows well indoors. For instance, most herbs will grow back after being clipped, but not cilantro and dill. Once you've clipped them down, you'll have to replant them. Basil is also more difficult to grow indoors because it wants lots of light and warmth.

Pots or Containers

Any time you choose a container for any plant, remember to make sure they have drainage holes!! Many herbs are native to semi-dry areas, and having a bunch of water collecting at the bottom of a pot with no drainage is a sure-fire way to kill off a plant.

Otherwise, you can go with any container with any material, just as long as it's not too big or too small for your herb, so it can grow comfortably.

As always, choose a soilless potting media. Don't use soil straight out of the garden. Even the lightest and fluffiest garden soil will quickly compact itself in the pot, and garden soil could possibly introduce diseases that your plant doesn't need. Potting media is sterile, so it doesn't harbor surprise disease or critters, and it's made with light materials that roots can easily tunnel through, such as coco coir, peat, perlite, as well as nutrients and minerals.

Light

Like many of the plants in this book, herbs need bright light with direct sun exposure for six to eight hours a day. If you have a south-facing window with lots of light, you should have it made. Be sure to turn the pot every couple of days so all parts of the plant are getting direct sun.

If you don't have a bright window, grow them under grow lights from about 12 to 16 hours a day. They should be between five to 15 inches from the light – any closer or further away, and the herbs won't thrive. You can set a clump of potted herb plants on the kitchen counter and attach several LED grow lights to the bottom of the shelves above them to give them the light they need.

Watering

Let your herbs dry out between waterings, and choose potting soil with good drainage. If you make your own potting soil, mix equal parts of sand, potting mix, peat moss, and perlite, and mix in a granular fertilizer like Osmocote.

Keep the temperature at about 70 degrees, and in winter, try to keep the humidity up by using either a humidifier, or the tray of-stones-with-water-in-them trick.

Be sure to keep trimming back the herbs as you use them to keep them branching out. Snip off flowers before they bloom, which makes them stop growing and takes the essential oils out of their leaves.

Fertilizing

Give them a low dose of water-soluble fertilizer twice a month. Heavier doses might weaken the flavor of the herbs.

Another good choice is compost tea. If you have a compost pile, there are a half-million ways to make compost tea. An easy-straightforward recipe would be to add a shovelful of compost to a 5-gallon bucket with non-chlorinated water (rainwater is good). Stir it and set it aside for a week, stirring once or twice a day. Using an old colander (please don't use the one out of the kitchen), strain the compost into a wide-mouthed jar or storage container. Dilute it with water, 1:1 if it's super-dark, then you can water your plants with it or even spray the foliage. If you have lots of plants to water, dilute it further. This is not a straight-up scientific recipe so you have plenty of wiggle room to play with it.

If this sounds like a lot, you can also buy compost tea bags online or at your local nursery. Again, keep these out of the kitchen!

Thus endeth the book on indoor gardening.

If you liked this book, do give me a review, and take a look at the next book, wherein we go back outside to grow our food.

PREORDER THE NEXT BOOK IN THE HUNGRY GARDEN SERIES

Growing a Food Forest: Trees, Shrubs, and Perennials That'll Feed Ya!

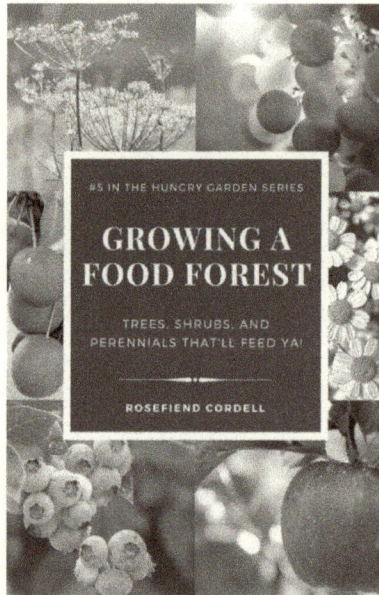

Preorder your copy here!
Out on 1 September 2023.
https://books2read.com/u/mV0wzp

OTHER BOOKS IN THE HUNGRY GARDEN SERIES

Little Pots, Big Yields: Container Gardening for Creative Gardeners

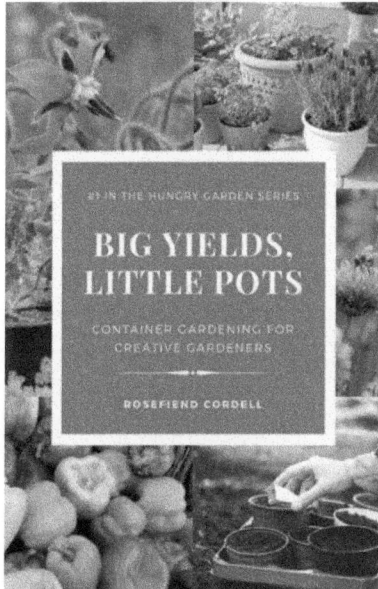

If you are short on space, or if you have the soil from hell, or if you have a hard time stooping and bending, then growing vegetables in containers is the solution for you. If you want to talk about improving the quality of your life, the fresh herbs and tomatoes and strawberries ripening on your balcony will do the job.

Your container vegetable garden will take a small investment of time and effort, but anything good does. Patience and practice in gardening will yield the best results.

This book covers:

* Choosing the right container
* How to start seeds (and combat damping-off disease)
* Soilless mixes and their elements
* Fertilizer, watering, climate, trellising

And this book will dig into the different kinds of vegetables that grow best in pots - best methods for each crop - best varieties for containers. This book is the essential guide to container gardening for beginners and also for seasoned gardeners who have been around the block a few times.

Edible Landscaping: Foodscaping and Permaculture for Urban Gardeners

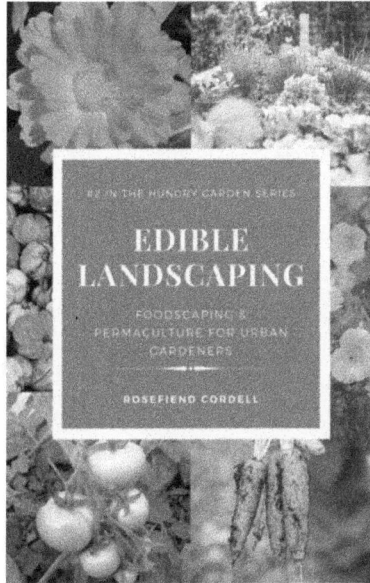

Liberate your food plants from the vegetable garden! Landscape your living space so it offers food for the eyes, heart, and stomach. Edible Landscaping: Foodscaping and Permaculture for Urban Gardeners is a how-to gardening manual written by a hard-boiled former horticulturist who hates weeding with the heat of a million suns. Rosefiend Cordell takes the budding gardener on a step-by-step process to transform their sad yard into a merry garden full of ornamental flowers linking arms with tomatoes, herbs, and edible flowers, as well as good fruit and nut trees.

This gardening book features practical gardening methods that help you create a design to build the outdoor living space you want. Information on foodscaping and permaculture, and how these techniques can help you to build the soil, prepare a garden design, and choose the plants you want.

Create a mixed border that cuddles herbs, edible flowers, vegetables, ornamental plants, and fruits together in harmony. It doesn't matter if you have a brown thumb or a green thumb. If you live in the city, the suburbs, or way out in the sticks, this handy-dandy manual will teach you how to make the best use of the space you have while opening your eyes to a great old way of gardening that's beautiful, tasty, and deeply satisfying.

Beneficial and Pest Insects – The Good, the Bad, and the Hungry

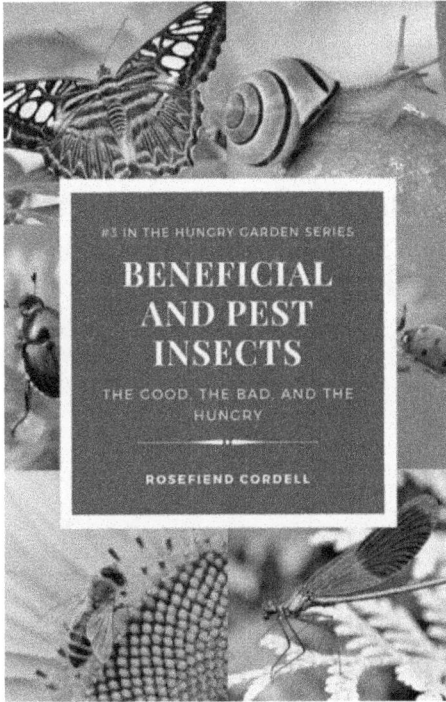

Book 3 of the Hungry Garden series talks about the other hungry species dwelling in your garden – insects! Whether they're eating your plants – or eating the insects that are eating your plants – insects are fascinating to learn about, even the garden-wreckers.

Learn to observe what lives on your roses, what's laying eggs on the underside of your tomato leaves, and what insects are lying in ambush for pests. This book will help you tell the helpful bugs from the harmful ones, and walk you through ways to encourage beneficial insects while discouraging the pests and helping you to limit pest damage.

This volume covers a plethora of beneficial insects, including damselflies, lacewings, ladybugs, wheel bugs and assassin bugs, praying mantis, big-eyed bugs, wasps, cicada killers, and leaf-cutter bees. It also has a rouge's gallery of pest insects: mealybugs, whiteflies, scale, stink bugs, fungus gnats, flea beetles, tomato hornworms, aphids, spotted cucumber beetles, spider mites, thrips, Japanese beetles, squash bugs, grasshoppers, and emerald ash borers. We also have ways you can control pests without harmful chemicals and sprays, and ways to attract your insect friends, create a habitat for beneficial insects, and make them happy in your garden.

INDOOR GARDENING

A PREVIEW OF THE EASY-GROWING GARDENING SERIES

The Easy-Growing Gardening series is 13 books written to help you navigate the garden. Need help with the rose garden? Growing perennials? Garden design? Vegetable gardening? Tomatoes? Are Japanese beetles getting you down? The Easy-Growing Gardening series will help you with these topics and more.

Sample Chapter from <u>Stay Grounded: Soil Building for Sustainable Gardens</u>

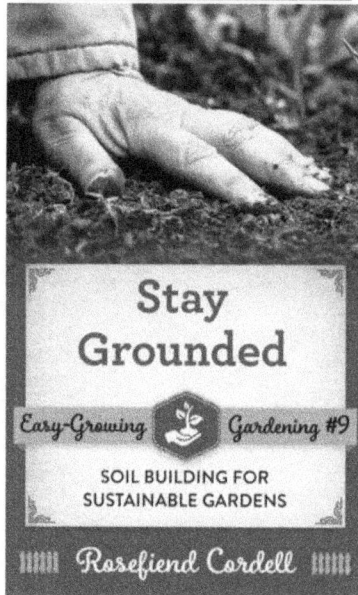

One of the most important things a gardener can do is to build up the soil in her garden. But keep in mind that soil-building is not a one-time operation – it's a process. As humus is devoured by

microorganisms, worms, and plants, more organic material must constantly be added in order to keep the soil biomass, and thereby the plants, well-fed and happy. Also, humus makes the soil porous and fluffy, builds a strong soil structure, and releases nutrients in a form that's easily absorbed by plant roots. Stay Grounded is your one-stop shop for soil building success.

SOIL BUILDING:
Saving the world, one dirt clod at a time.

One of the most important things a gardener can do is to build up the soil in her garden. But keep in mind that soil-building is not a one-time operation – it's a process. As humus is devoured by microorganisms, worms, and plants, more organic material must constantly be added in order to keep the soil biomass, and thereby the plants, well-fed and happy. Also, humus makes the soil porous and fluffy, builds a strong soil structure, and releases nutrients in a form that's easily absorbed by plant roots.

Chemical fertilizers will not add humus to the soil. These are merely nutritional supplements; plants and their soil need real food – organic material.

But so much good organic material never makes it back into the soil. Leaves, grass clippings, and yard waste ends up choking our landfills instead of nourishing the ground. This is wrong.

Mulch the world!

I have a fairly simple way to deal with weeds: mulch. I like to take newspapers, ten pages at a time, and lay them over the garden, making sure there's enough overlap between each section so light won't get down to the soil. Then I throw straw, grass clippings, leafmould, or whatever on top to make it all tidy and neat.

The neat thing with the newspapers is that you can get a ton of them for your purposes for free, simply by asking your neighbors or by picking them up at the local library. Also, you can lay these newspapers right over the weeds and you never hear another peep out of them for the rest of the year. Even when you have tall grass or weeds up to a foot tall, stomp them down, or mow them, before putting the newspapers on top. They get smothered right out.

The newspapers will also break down and add valuable organic material to the soil. You can lay your tomatoes right on top. You won't have to wipe the dirt off your low-hanging fruits any more. Nice, huh?

Use those leaves!

Next, use leaves and excess grass clippings in the garden. Fifteen big bags of leaves, when chewed up by a lawnmower, turn into an inch of mulch on a 15 by 25' garden. (The job took about 30 or 45 minutes.) I did that last fall; this spring, I'm finding worm castings all over!

Pour the leaves out on your garden, mow them into little pieces, and till them under. Or leave them on top of the soil and don't bother tilling. With mulch, you don't have to worry about your garden drying out – or weeds coming up.

If you don't have leaves, take a trip to the local landfill and get some. There's usually a separate area for yard waste, and there the leaves are free for the taking. (Be careful with grass clippings, because they sometimes contain herbicides.) Or grab bags of leaves off the curb before the garbage truck arrives. Or get them from your neighbors; they're always glad to have them taken off their hands.

Earthworms = earth movers

The more I read about earthworms and observe them, the more I am convinced that these creatures are a blessing to the soil. They bring up valuable nutrients from the subsoil, their castings are among the best plant food, their tunnels bring air (which is rich in nitrogen) into the ground. Plant roots even seek out earthworm burrows for the nutrients they contain.

Nightcrawlers are best for this work. The red worms, or red wrigglers, prefer to live in compost and leafmould; they're good for mixing up cool compost piles but will not dig very far into the soil. Nightcrawlers will dig burrows deep into the ground, which is what you want.

After it rains, pick earthworms off the sidewalks to put in the garden. Or, go to the bait shop and get them there. See if they'll throw in some egg cases with your worm purchase, because if all the worms don't survive, the egg cases will.

Dump a couple of worms out in various places around the garden and cover them with a little soil so they can get underground before the sun and wind dries them out. They generally will get underground within the hour, even on really cold days.

I generally put worms out in the garden every spring. Twelve to 24 worms would probably be good for a small garden, twice that for big gardens.

Green manures

Green manures such as buckwheat, clovers, lespedeza, or oats can be grown between rows, under tall plants, or at season's end all over the garden. In any case, they're tilled under three weeks before a new crop is seeded to allow them to decompose. It's a valuable way to get fast organic material.

Use green manures fill in where a crop has finished. For example, once the spinach is all picked, throw down some rye seeds or white clover to fill the area in until next spring. Chickpeas make a nice cover crop, and they're edible, and they add much-needed nitrogen to the soil. Daikon radishes are good, too.

Grow legumes as an understory to your hungry corn crop. Leave enough space between the corn rows in order to run a lawnmower between the rows. This will keep the cover crop nice, neat, and low, and the clippings will provide lots of nitrogen-rich mulch for the rest of the garden.

Alfalfa is great for walkways because its clippings, as they break down, release a chemical called triacontanol that acts as a growth stimulant to plants. A small amount of alfalfa clippings can increase vegetable yields by 30 to 60 percent. And those alfalfa roots go deep into the subsoil, pulling up nutrients from deep underground, breaking up soil, and fixing nitrogen.

If you don't want to plant alfalfa, but you want its benefits, you can purchase alfalfa meal at feed stores or order it online. Scatter it over the soil according to package directions to improve growth. Don't spread it too heavily because it will mat and shed water.

Compost

Compost is a fine way to recycle kitchen and garden scraps into fertilizer. And it's earthworm heaven.

Kitchen scraps that are good for compost include such things as fruit and vegetable remains, eggshells, and bread. It's not a good idea to put meat products or leftover milk products in a compost pile (unless it's a very hot pile) due to the possiblities of it attracting dogs and cats. Also it could smell bad. However, if you've been fishing, you can bury the fish bits in the soil. Fish bits are high in nitrogen, and they will make your corn plants love you.

I generally throw my compostables onto the garden during the winter, and put them on the compost pile during the rest of the year. I've heard that compostables on the ground attract mice. But in deep winter they'll also attract songbirds, which is nice. (It's always fun to throw popcorn out to see what kinds of birds I get.)

Some people also dig small holes into particularly infertile areas of the garden, drop compostables into it until it's nearly full, then close it up and start a new one. This doesn't work so well in desert soils – produce buried in sandy soils has been dug up a month later, looking as fresh as it did when it had been buried.

My soil is evil!

Sometimes you get soil that has basically been created by Satan. Examples of evil soil include subdivision soil – that pasty clay that's created by heavy equipment churning up soil, wet or dry, and compacting it into concrete. Or you have desert asphalt, or fragipan, or stuff you have to take a jackhammer to.

Raised beds are always a good idea here. Lay a thick layer of newspapers over the ground, make an enclosure, then it fill up with compost, rotted manure, and topsoil brought in from elsewhere. Go heavy on the compost! Grow a hedge of deep-rooted legumes around the outside of the enclosure, and underplant tall vegetables (like corn) with small legumes such as white clover. Release nightcrawlers into the soil. This will give you a place to plant while you wait for the compost and the earthworms to do their work on the soil underneath.

Every year, try to mix the good soil in a little bit more, by double digging, or, if that's not working, even by moving aside the top layer of the soil and working a garden fork into the bad soil to aerate it. Keep laying down the organic material, though. Here, more than anything else, soilbuilding is a process. It will take several years of hard work to bring a dead soil back to life, so be patient.

But a living soil is the best soil for all. So keep at it.

So, keep adding humus in every way, shape, and form you can think of to keep the garden happy and to keep the soil biomass active. This will make an incredible difference in your garden – one you'll definitely love.

USDA PLANT HARDINESS ZONE MAP

Now and then I mention what zone a plant is hardy to. For those of you who reside in the United States, the hardiness zone is depicted on this map, and shows the high and low temperatures of the area where you live. This map is from 2012, and as you know, climate change is still throwing this thing off to some extent, and will be changing it more over in upcoming years. But it's still helpful.

The USDA has this map on their website, but if you go there, you can click on your state to get a closer view of what your particular zone looks like. Go to their website over here at https://plianthardiness.ars.usda.gov/PHZMWeb/ to get started.

Me with two baby chickies, my laptop, and a can of Red Bull.
This is how I roll, people.

ABOUT THE AUTHOR

A former city horticulturist and a long-time garden writer, Rosefiend Cordell, aka Melinda R. Cordell, has written 12 books in the Easy-Growing Gardening series under the name Rosefiend Cordell, and three books (so far) in the Hungry Garden series.

She's worked in horticulture for half of her life – longer if you count when she was young, collecting wildflowers. She's worked in greenhouses, both retail and commercial; as a landscape laborer and designer; as a perennials manager; as municipal horticulturist and public rose garden potentate; and now as a gardening author (which is much easier on the back and joints).

Melinda R. Cordell has written a truckload of YA novels, including the Dragonriders of Fiorenza series. Set in an alternative medieval Italy, it features a wily dragonrider, her loyal dragon, and her assassin grandma, all pitted against a world out to strip away every last one of their hopes and dreams.

Melinda lives in northwest Missouri with her husband and two kids, the best little family to walk the earth, and is writing about 24 books at once, fueled by passion and caffeine.

If you want to keep up with her, you can drop her a friendly note at rosefiend@gmail.com.

Don't forget to leave a book review on your favorite retailer, BookBub, or Goodreads!

melindacordell.com

INDOOR GARDENING

www.ingramcontent.com/pod-product-compliance
Lightning Source LLC
Chambersburg PA
CBHW030841090426
42737CB00009B/1059